The Genius of
American Corporate Law

T0272896

AEI STUDIES IN REGULATION AND FEDERALISM
Christopher C. DeMuth and Jonathan R. Macey, series editors

Costly Policies: State Regulation and Antitrust Exemption
in Insurance Markets
Jonathan R. Macey and Geoffrey P. Miller

Federalism in Taxation: The Case for Greater Uniformity
Daniel Shaviro

The Genius of American Corporate Law
Roberta Romano

Product-Risk Labeling: A Federal Responsibility
W. Kip Viscusi

State and Federal Regulation of National Advertising
J. Howard Beales and Timothy J. Muris

The Genius of
American Corporate Law

Roberta Romano

The AEI Press

Publisher for the American Enterprise Institute
WASHINGTON, D.C.

1993

Distributed to the Trade by National Book Network, 15200 NBN Way, Blue Ridge
Summit, PA 17214. To order call toll free 1-800-462-6420 or 1-717-794-3800.
For all other inquiries please contact the AEI Press, 1150 Seventeenth Street, N.W.,
Washington, D.C. 20036 or call 1-800-862-5801.

Library of Congress Cataloging-in-Publication Data

Romano, Roberta.
    The genius of American corporate law / Roberta Romano.
       p.   cm.—(AEI studies in regulation and federalism)
    ISBN 0-8447-3837-9.—ISBN 0-8447-3836-0 (pbk.)
    1. Corporation law—United States. I. Title. II. Series.
    KF1414.R65   1993
    346.73'066—dc20
    [347.30666]   93-18917
                                              CIP
    ISBN 978-0-8447-3836-9

    3   5   7   9   10   8   6   4

© 1993 by the American Enterprise Institute for Public Policy Research, Washington,
D.C. All rights reserved. No part of this publication may be used or reproduced in any
manner whatsoever without permission in writing from the American Enterprise
Institute except in the case of brief quotations embodied in news articles, critical
articles, or reviews. The views expressed in the publications of the American
Enterprise Institute are those of the authors and do not necessarily reflect the view of
the staff, advisory panels, officers, or trustees of AEI.

THE AEI PRESS
Publisher for the American Enterprise Institute
1150 17th Street, N.W., Washington, D.C. 20036

Printed in the United States of America

Contents

A Note about the Book

ROBERTA ROMANO'S study of American corporate law is one of a series of research monographs commissioned by the American Enterprise Institute's Regulation and Federalism Project. The purpose of the project is to examine the advantages and disadvantages of American federalism in important areas of contemporary business regulation, including product labeling, advertising, insurance, transportation, communications, and environmental quality.

The benefits of state autonomy—diversity, responsiveness to local circumstances, and constraint on the power of the national government—are fundamental to the American political creed and deeply embedded in our political institutions. Are these benefits real and substantial in the case of business regulation? How do they compare with the costs of duplication, inconsistency, and interference with free interstate commerce that state regulation can entail? Has the growth of national and international commerce altered the balance of federalism's benefits and costs—for example, by affecting the ability of individual states to pursue local policies at the expense of citizens of other states? Are there practical means of reducing the economic costs of state autonomy in regulation while preserving its political benefits?

The authors of these volumes have found different answers to these questions in the context of different markets and regulatory regimes: they call for greater national uniformity in some cases, greater state autonomy in others, and a revision of the rules of state "policy competition" in still others. We hope that this research will be useful to officials and legislators at all levels of government and to the business executives who must live with their policies. More generally, we hope that the AEI project will prove to be a significant contribution to our understanding of one of the most distinctive and important features of American government.

AEI is delighted to be publishing Professor Romano's study as part of this series. She has been, as Judge Winter notes in his foreword, a leader of the revolution in academic thinking and research regarding the nature and consequences of corporate law. Judge Winter omits to mention only that he himself incited this revolution, in his professorial days, through his academic writing and a landmark AEI monograph, *Government and the Corporation*, published in 1978. In the 1980s, Professor Romano refined, extended, and gave full empirical structure to Judge Winter's original insights. *The Genius of American Corporate Law* consolidates and elaborates this work; it is a worthy successor to *Government and the Corporation* and testimony to the power of careful research to untangle complex and controversial policy questions.

Each of the monographs produced for the Regulation and Federalism Project was discussed and criticized at an AEI seminar involving federal and state lawmakers, business executives, professionals, and academic experts with a wide range of interests and viewpoints. I would like to thank all of them for their contributions, noting, however, that final exposition and conclusions were entirely the work of the authors of each monograph. I am particularly grateful to Jonathan R. Macey of Cornell University and Heather Gradison of AEI, who organized and directed the project's research and seminars along with me, and to John D. Ong and Jon V. Heider of the BFGoodrich Company and Patricia H. Engman of the Business Roundtable, who suggested the project in the first place, worked hard and effectively to raise financial support for it, and provided valuable counsel and encouragement throughout.

CHRISTOPHER C. DeMUTH
President, American Enterprise Institute
for Public Policy Research

Foreword

THE GENIUS OF AMERICAN CORPORATE LAW typifies a revolution in academic discourse regarding corporate law. Twenty years ago, it would have been inconceivable that a scholar such as Roberta Romano—renowned for her rigorous empirical testing, and thoughtful application, of theory—would publish a work with such a title. Twenty years ago, legal scholars were herdlike in regarding corporate law as a species of consumer protection in which the law's role was to protect helpless investors by hogtying a predatory corporate management. For example, in 1976, Richard Jennings, a well-known professor of corporate law, stated that it was "common knowledge"[1] among legal scholars that state corporate codes exploited equity investors for the benefit of corporate management and that federal regulation, in particular a law requiring the federal chartering of corporations, was necessary. In the same year, a petition to the Congress calling for federal chartering legislation was signed by eighty professors from sixty-two law schools.[2] This view was echoed in article after article by professors from leading law schools calling for stringent federal laws regulating the conduct of corporate management.

Today, as Professor Romano's work demonstrates, the academic discourse is vastly different, drawing on transaction-costs economics and the efficient market hypothesis, explaining legal rules in terms of agency costs, examining diversification as a market-oriented means of investors protecting themselves, and generally focusing on the

---

1. Richard W. Jennings, "Federalization of Corporate Law: Part Way or All the Way," *Business Lawyer*, vol. 31 (1976), p. 991.

2. Letter submitted by David L. Chambers, in U.S. Congress, Senate, *Corporate Rights and Responsibilities: Hearings before the Senate Committee on Commerce*, 94th Congress, 2d session, 1976, p. 343.

interrelationships of legal rules and market forces in monitoring management and enhancing corporate performance. As in any revolution, the participants are far more united in their condemnation of the *ancien régime* than in their view of the new world. Thus the newer scholars debate the merits of legal rules compelling auctions in takeover situations, prohibitions on insider trading (somehow defined), and the degree to which state chartering of corporations yields efficient rules. Nevertheless, the discussion has moved to a higher plane.

The revolution, at least among the legal professoriate, began with the application of a simple economic proposition: in any consensual commercial transaction, the parties need each other. The earlier critics ignored this by implicitly assuming that investors were at the mercy of management. Judge Frank H. Easterbrook has accurately described these critics as "see[ing] the world as if everyone awakened one morning to find himself a manager or an investor. The veil of ignorance was suddenly parted. The manager stepped out and exalted: 'Aha! No one can stop me!' The investor gasped: 'Woe is me, I'm powerless. Only the ALI [American Law Institute] can save me now!' "[3]

Once the silliness of the critics' assumption was exposed, the world of legal commentary had to change. Corporate management is constantly in search of fresh capital. Investors do not have to select the debt or equity offerings of any particular firm. They do not even have to invest in firms but rather can choose real estate, government securities, precious metals, race horses, or what have you. This dose of economic reality, which suggests that large investors are hardly helpless, thank you, and small investors can protect themselves against many risks by diversification, rendered most of the earlier criticism obsolete. In particular, it undermined the view that state corporate law was the product of a "race to the bottom."

The most cited basis for the race-to-the-bottom argument was an article by Professor William Cary of Columbia Law School,[4] which

---

3. Frank H. Easterbrook, "Managers' Discretion and Investors' Welfare: Theories and Evidence," *Delaware Journal of Corporate Law*, vol. 9 (1984), pp. 540, 542.

4. William L. Cary, "Federalism and Corporate Law: Reflections upon Delaware," *Yale Law Journal*, vol. 83 (1974), p. 663.

was widely perceived as the most influential piece ever published by the *Yale Law Journal*.[5] The article was so highly regarded that the American Bar Association's Committee on Federal Regulation of Securities conducted a symposium that used it as the basis for discussion; the proceedings were published in *Business Lawyer*.[6] Cary's thesis was that the competition of states for corporate charters led to codes that allowed management to siphon earnings—a noncompetitive return—to itself. As Professor Romano demonstrates, however, the race-to-the-bottom argument is almost surely wrong. If corporate management is regularly in search of fresh capital and investors need not select business firms, much less firms chartered in a particular state, corporations governed by a legal system that deliberately seeks to diminish that yield must pay more for capital. A legal system that systematically seeks to diminish, or even risks diminishing, the yield to investors is thus self-defeating, because investors will be deterred by the simplest of calculations—a comparison of earnings between corporations.

This is not to say that state corporate codes are always efficient. As Professor Romano indicates, for example, state antitakeover statutes are inefficient. Such laws, however, are largely not the result of state competition for corporate charters but are generally passed at the behest of a particular business rather than to increase revenues from chartering. In identifying the competition between states for corporate charters as a problem, Professor Cary was thus wrong. The problem is not that states compete for charters but that too often they do not. What Professor Cary saw as a fault is in fact "the genius of American corporate law."

The theoretical implications of recognizing Cary's error are profound. By creating a market for legal rules and allowing corporations to select the legal system that will govern their internal affairs, a mechanism has been created with the potential of relieving us of a significant number of judgment calls about the substance of corporate law. So long as states compete for charters, any rule that results in a

---

5. Cf. Fred R. Shapiro, "The Most-Cited Articles from the Yale Law Journal," *Yale Law Journal*, vol. 100 (1991), p. 1449 (listing Cary's article as one of the *Journal's* most cited articles, with 211 citations).

6. *Business Lawyer*, 1976, pp. 863, 883.

net increase in corporate charters issued by a state can be presumed to be an efficient rule. The intended jibe, "law for sale," is thus a compliment.

The practical implications of seeing the error in the race-to-the-bottom argument, however, are considerably less grandiose. First, the state race for charters may not be even a sprint, much less a marathon. If Delaware is the only state that raises a significant portion of its tax revenues from charters, the organized bar may be the only political force in other states pressing for efficient rules. If so, Delaware need be only marginally more efficient than the others.[7] Second, inefficient rules that attract reincorporation (after some investors are locked in), such as an antitakeover law, may sometimes lead to a net increase in tax revenue. Whether this is frequent is unclear.[8]

Professor Romano's work demonstrates that the academic analysis of corporate law has been significantly altered in yet another way. Ever since Berle and Means,[9] the central issue of corporate law has been how to create a legal structure that monitors management. The earlier critics seemed consumed by a concern that legal rules were so lax that management would be susceptible to routine negligence or would take advantage of its position to conduct corporate affairs for management's personal profit. Today, the newer scholars perceive the problem as one of increasing management's productivity in ways not susceptible to enhancement by legal mandates or prohibitions based on the duty of care and the duty of loyalty. We simply cannot command individuals by law to be effective managers. Indeed, given that shareholders can diversify against the risk of inaccurate decisions or even negligence, there is a serious question whether a stringent duty of care is less efficient than no duty of care. (Delaware now allows corporate charters to limit liability for violations of the duty of care.)[10] In fact, there is reason to believe that management's large investment of its human capital in one firm causes it to be over-

---

7. Ralph K. Winter, "The Race for the Top Revisited: A Comment on Eisenberg," *Columbia Law Journal*, vol. 89 (1989), pp. 1526, 1529.

8. Ibid., p. 1528.

9. Adolph A. Berle and Gardiner C. Means, *The Modern Corporation and Private Property* (1933).

10. Del. Code Ann. tit. 8, § 102(b)(7) (Supp. 1992).

cautious, a tendency that would be aggravated by a rule that penalized seemingly risky decisions. With regard to the duty of loyalty, a rule against outright self-dealing may be sufficient to allow shareholders to achieve protection through diversification.

As *The Genius of American Corporate Law* makes clear, the incentives created by legal structures are more important than rules seeking to regulate behavior directly. What is needed is a legal structure that frees shareholders and the capital market to monitor management. This means less regulation rather than more. Laws and regulations that prevent the purchase of large blocs of stock or inhibit large shareholders from collectively monitoring management should be reconsidered. Similarly, the Williams Act, state antitakeover laws, and court decisions allowing management to prevent the alienation of shares in control transactions all reduce the effectiveness of the capital market in monitoring management's behavior.

At stake is the capacity of American firms to compete in world markets. Protectionist legal rules preventing monitoring by large shareholders or by the market for management control impede that competition. Ironically, such rules do not permanently protect inefficient managements but rather allow them to stay in place while their companies face a long decline. The rules merely prolong the illness by preventing the cure, while those who depend on the firms for their livelihood suffer unnecessarily.

The Genius of American Corporate Law is thus a superb work that builds on and furthers our understanding of the relationship of law and markets to corporate performance. It is a major event in an intellectual revolution in which Roberta Romano's place is both important and secure.

RALPH K. WINTER
Circuit Judge
U.S. Court of Appeals
for the Second Circuit

Acknowledgments

I HAVE HAD THE GOOD FORTUNE to have outstanding teachers. First, I am a member of the generation of Yale Law School students who had the privilege of being introduced to corporate finance by Marvin Chirelstein. He is a master teacher, and that course, with the nondescript title of Business Units II, sparked my research interest in corporate law. Then, at Stanford Law School, I was extraordinarily lucky to have Myron Scholes as a colleague. I learned from him the use of applied corporate finance for answering policy questions and the importance of combining a firm grounding in finance theory with a mastery of the institutional terrain. At that time, another colleague, Bob Ellickson, was beginning work on his now-classic case study of cattle ranching in Shasta County and the Coase theorem. He taught me that there is as much to learn from the world outside the law school library as within it, impressing on me the importance of field research. Finally, Oliver Williamson, through his writings and for too brief a period of time as a colleague at Yale, shaped my thinking on business organization. I am deeply grateful to them all for educating me and for their friendship. I am certain that they would not concur with all the conclusions in this monograph, and they are, of course, not responsible for the product. But to the extent there is value added to our understanding of corporate law by my work, they significantly contributed to its creation.

I have received helpful comments on drafts of the monograph from Ian Ayres, Theo Baums, Boris Bittker, Ron Daniels, Judge Frank Easterbrook, Henry Hansmann, Marcel Kahan, Michael Klausner, Fritz Kubler, Jonathan Macey, Jeff MacIntosh, Henry Manne, Richard Revesz, Peter Schuck, Greg Sidak, and Ed Zelinsky. I also received valuable feedback while presenting all or part of drafts of the monograph at the following institutions: University of Alberta Faculty of Law (John A. Weir Memorial Lecture); American Enterprise

Institute; Duquesne University School of Law; Fordham University School of Law (Robert L. Levine Lecture); Tulane University Department of Economics and Newcomb Foundation; Yale Law School; and Yale School of Organization and Management. A version of chapter 4 titled "Competition for Corporate Charters and the Lesson of Takeover Statutes" was published in the *Fordham Law Review* (March 1993). Some passages of that chapter also appeared in "Rethinking Takeover Regulation," *Journal of Applied Corporate Finance*, volume 5 (Fall 1992).

Finally, I would like to express my gratitude to Chris DeMuth not only for his careful editing and commentary, which improved the manuscript, but also for suggesting that I write this AEI monograph as a forum for my view of the dynamics of American corporate law, to reach a far broader audience than professional journals would.

About the Author

ROBERTA ROMANO is Allen Duffy/Class of 1960 Professor of Law at the Yale Law School and an adjunct scholar at the American Enterprise Institute. Her research has focused on state competition for corporate charters, the political economy of takeover regulation, shareholder litigation, and pension fund activities in corporate governance. She is series editor for Oxford University Press's Interdisciplinary Readers in Law Series and the editor of a volume in the series, *Foundations of Corporate Law* (1993). From 1988 to 1992, she was coeditor of the *Journal of Law, Economics, and Organization*. Professor Romano now serves as a member of its editorial board, as well as the boards of the *Supreme Court Economic Review* and *Journal of Corporate Finance*. She is also a director of the American Law and Economics Association and chair-elect of the Law and Economics Section of the Association of American Law Schools.

Professor Romano received her B.A. with highest honors and distinction from the University of Rochester in 1973, her M.A. from the University of Chicago in 1975, and her J.D. from Yale Law School in 1980. She was a law clerk to Judge Jon O. Newman of the U.S. Court of Appeals for the Second Circuit, 1980–1981, and taught at Stanford Law School, 1981–1985, before joining the Yale faculty.

The Genius of
American Corporate Law

1
Introduction

THE GENIUS OF AMERICAN CORPORATE LAW is in its feder-
alist organization. In the United States, corporate law, which concerns the relation between a firm's shareholders and managers, is
largely a matter for the states. Firms choose their state of incorporation, a statutory domicile that is independent of physical presence
and that can be changed with shareholder approval. The legislative
approach is, in the main, enabling. Corporation codes supply standard contract terms for corporate governance. These terms function
as default provisions in corporate charters that firms can tailor more
precisely to their needs. Firms therefore can particularize their
charters under a state code, as well as seek the state whose code best
matches their needs so as to minimize their cost of doing business.

Provisions in corporation codes run the gamut from trivial
housekeeping to the fundamental fashioning of shareholder-manager
relations. They range from specifying that a corporation's name be
placed in its charter to specifying fiduciary duties of managers and
voting rights of shareholders, and when they can be waived, and
procedures for corporate combinations, including when managers' as
opposed to shareholders' decisions are controlling. States provide a
different set of governance defaults for small, privately held firms,
which are called close corporation codes. The variety in corporation
codes and in their enabling approach readily accommodates the
diversity in organization, capital structure, and lines of business
among business firms.

The master problem animating corporation codes is the separation of ownership from control in the modern public corporation.
Large firms typically have numerous shareholders with small holdings
who cannot actively exercise control over the firm or monitor management. The holdings of managers running such firms are also usually

1

infinitesimal. This creates an agency problem, in which the managers' operation of a firm may deviate from the shareholders' wishes to maximize the firm's value. Managers, for example, may implement a policy that makes their jobs more secure, such as engaging in defensive tactics to thwart a corporate takeover, even though the policy reduces the firm's value. Or, because the bulk of the managers' wealth is tied up in the firm in present and future compensation, they may adopt a corporate strategy that reduces firm-specific risk, such as diversifying corporate acquisitions, even though shareholders do not benefit from the policy because they hold diversified stock portfolios that are subject to market, and not firm-specific, risk. A primary function of corporation codes in this regard is to establish corporate governance devices that can mitigate the agency problem by better aligning manager incentives with shareholder interests. The more prominent examples of such devices are (1) shareholder-elected boards of directors who monitor managers, (2) shareholder voting rights for fundamental corporate changes, and (3) fiduciary duties that impose liability on managers and directors who act negligently or with divided loyalty (favoring their own financial interest over that of shareholders).

Corporate law presumes that firms should be managed for shareholders', and not managers', interests when those interests conflict. Profit maximization (in a world where cash flows are uncertain, this is equivalent to maximizing equity share prices) is the goal. There are a number of persuasive explanations for this perspective. First, in competitive markets, maximizing share value allocates resources efficiently and thereby maximizes social welfare.[1] Second, in competitive markets, it provides managers with a clear-cut decision rule that maximizes the utility of the firm's owners who may have disparate preferences for current and future consumption, because it enables shareholders to trade against the increased share value to

---

1. A profit-maximizing firm produces up to the point where price equals marginal cost (the cost of a unit of extra output), which is the point where an additional unit of output wastes resources, because the cost of producing that extra unit is greater than its value (the price consumers are willing to pay for it). Readers interested in the formal derivation of this result in welfare economics should consult an economics text, such as Hal R. Varian, *Microeconomic Analysis*, 3rd ed. (New York: W. W. Norton, 1992), pp. 215–29, 338–56.

achieve whatever consumption pattern they wish without affecting the firm's policy.[2] In this regard, it also reduces the cost of collective decisions, because shareholders' interests are more homogeneous than other groups.[3] Finally, it best matches organizational design with incentives. Because equity investments are residual claims with no fixed income guarantee or maturity date, they are the only investments in the firm that are not periodically renewed: hence, they are more vulnerable than the investments of other stakeholders, such as bondholders and employees, which can be and are protected by express contracting.[4]

National Controls

In addition to state corporation codes, shareholder-manager relations in public corporations are also subject to an array of national controls under the federal securities laws, which regulate the issuance and trading of securities and the continuing disclosure responsibilities to investors of public firms.[5] In contrast to state corporation laws, federal regulations are mandatory. The reach of federal securities laws into traditional spheres of state jurisdiction, such as officers' and directors' fiduciary duties to shareholders, has over time been expanded and contracted, like an accordion, by federal courts. But even here the national legislation is not preemptive: it expressly preserves a role for states in securities regulation. The relation,

2. See, for example, Richard Brealey and Stewart Myers, *Principles of Corporate Finance*, 4th ed. (New York: McGraw Hill, 1991), p. 22.

3. Henry Hansmann, "Ownership of the Firm," *Journal of Law, Economics, and Organization*, vol. 4 (1988), p. 267.

4. Oliver E. Williamson, "Corporate Governance," *Yale Law Journal*, vol. 93 (1984), p. 1197. Protective covenants, for example, are more readily specified in bondholders' than in shareholders' investment contracts, and workers are better protected from arbitrary dismissal or wage reduction through agreements negotiated by collective bargaining and by employment statutes than by representation on a corporate board.

5. Securities Exchange Act of 1934, 15 U.S.C. § 78a et seq.; Securities Act of 1933, 15 U.S.C. § 77a et seq. Corporate organization is affected by other areas of federal legislation, such as tax, environmental, and employment laws. These areas are outside the scope of this monograph.

however, is one-sided; the federal securities regime establishes minimum disclosure requirements, which states can expand but not diminish.

In contrast to the regime of disclosure under federal securities laws, many states engage in merit regulation. In such states, state officials must be satisified with the investment merits of a security before it can be sold. For state securities regulation, jurisdiction is derived from the location of the securities transaction, not the issuer's domicile. State intrusion into the governance of foreign corporations (the term of art for a corporation not incorporated in the state)[6] through securities regulation is limited, however; large public corporations are typically exempt from state securities regulation.[7] Hence, in the accommodation concerning corporate law struck by American federalism, the national government has left considerable latitude to the states. Many commentators on corporate law view this balance as troubling. Some advocate national preemption of state corporation codes; others, preemption of state securities regulation.[8] This monograph contends that such perspectives on corporate law are mistaken.

Federalism and Corporate Law

A federal system of government produces a number of benefits for its citizens. It protects the individual from the immense power of government, as the states are a counterweight to the national government.[9] It can allocate public goods and services more efficiently, as

---

6. Because the term "foreign corporation" is applied to any corporation not incorporated locally in a state, it refers to U.S. corporations: for example, a corporation incorporated in Delaware is a foreign corporation to any of the other forty-nine states.

7. State and federal securities regulation is discussed in chapter 5.

8. For example, Donald Schwartz, "A Case for Federal Chartering of Corporations," *Business Lawyer*, vol. 31 (1976), p. 1125; Rutherford B. Campbell, "An Open Attack on the Nonsense of Blue Sky Regulation," *Journal of Corporation Law*, vol. 10 (1985), p. 553.

9. This insight is not new to the federalism debate; see, for example, Alexis de Tocqueville, *Democracy in America* (1835), edited by R. Heffner (New York: New American Library, 1956). Wherever possible, I refer to the federal government as the national government to avoid confusion of the two common usages of the term "federal" as describing (1) the central or national government and (2) a federal

well as increase individual utility, compared with a centralized government because of its superior ability to match specific government policies with diverse citizen preferences regarding such policies: in a federal system, states and municipalities compete for citizens who choose to reside in the jurisdiction offering their preferred package of public goods and services.[10] Finally, federalism spurs innovation in public policy because of the incremental experimentation afforded by fifty laboratories of states competing for citizens and firms.[11] A policy improvement identified by one state is quickly enacted by other states.[12]

But just as the benefits from federalism are axiomatic in American politics, it is also well recognized that a federal system can impede the administration of government and thereby diminish individual welfare. In particular, if the costs and benefits of a specific public policy do not fall within the boundaries of one jurisdiction, the optimal quantity and quality of public goods and services will not be produced. A state will not want to pay for benefits experienced by nonresidents, for example, and thus will underprovide a public good or service (such as a mosquito-spraying program that will benefit adjoining jurisdictions or highways that are used by interstate travelers). Similarly, states may export the cost of providing goods and services for their residents to nonresidents, for instance, by adopting taxes that are more likely to be paid by out-of-state than in-state individuals or firms—severance taxes in natural resource states, gaming taxes in Nevada, and in Iowa a single-factor corporate tax

---

system of government, in which the states share power with the national government. Where it is clear from the context, I will continue to use the term "federal" in the first sense, as, for example, in referring to federal securities laws.

10. The classic article is Charles Tiebout, "A Pure Theory of Local Expenditures," *Journal of Political Economy*, vol. 64 (1956), p. 416.

11. Recent discussions of the benefits and costs of federalism include Thomas R. Dye, *American Federalism: Competition among Governments* (Lexington, Mass.: Lexington Books, 1990), and the essays in Daphne A. Kenyon and John Kincaid, eds., *Competition among States and Local Governments* (Washington, D.C.: Urban Institute, 1991).

12. A brief summary of numerous studies of diffusion of legislative and other public policy measures across the states can be found in Albert Breton, "The Existence and Stability of Interjurisdictional Competition," in Kenyon and Kincaid, *Competition among States and Local Governments*, pp. 38–40.

formula based on sales, which gives advantages to local firms that sell the bulk of their products out of state. [13]

A more adverse consequence of federalism is the potential for interjurisdictional competition that is not even zero-sum but a negative-sum game. Many commentators have characterized state economic development policies as such a game, in which competing states offer subsidies to firms that exceed the revenue from the local jobs they create. [14] Finally, by tolerating overlapping jurisdictional authority or requiring intergovernmental coordination, federalism raises the cost of implementing public policy, even when there is consensus on the policy objective.

The corporate law literature is a microcosm of this tension in the policy debate over federalism because an important theme in the literature focuses on the effect of competition among the states for tax revenues generated by corporate charters. Corporation codes can be viewed as products, whose producers are states and whose consumers are corporations. A key question is whether there is any reason to suppose that the code provisions produced by state competition benefit investors. The concern arises because one state within the federal structure, Delaware, which is a small state by any measure—population, geography, industrial or agricultural production—has dominated all the rest.

Delaware and Competition for State Charters

Approximately one-half of the largest industrial firms are incorporated in Delaware, and of the corporations listed on national exchanges, more are incorporated in Delaware than in any other state. Moreover, the vast majority of reincorporating firms move to Delaware. As a result, a substantial portion of the state's tax revenue—averaging more than 15 percent from 1960 to 1990—is derived from incorporation fees (table 1–1). While the absolute dollars raised from

---

13. U.S. Advisory Committee on Intergovernmental Relations, *Interjurisdictional Tax and Policy Competition: Good or Bad for the Federal System?* (Washington, D.C.: ACIR, April 1991), pp. 36–37.

14. See Daphne A. Kenyon and John Kincaid, "Introduction," in Kenyon and Kincaid, eds., *Competition among States and Local Governments*, pp. 22–23.

TABLE 1–1
FINANCING DELAWARE'S CHARTERING BUSINESS, 1960–1990

Year	Estimated Cost[a] ($)	Franchise Tax Revenues ($)	Franchise Tax as % of Total Tax Collected
1960	353,870	9,864,000	13.7
1961	336,870	12,621,000	16.3
1962	418,430	13,579,000	14.9
1963	440,325	13,977,000	14.3
1964	479,080	15,635,000	15.5
1965	476,380	15,790,000	13.1
1966	492,400	14,091,000	10.9
1967	516,700	17,615,000	12.6
1968	606,322	21,414,000	14.8
1969	644,470	20,572,000	13.1
1970	721,500	43,924,000	22.5
1971	835,900	55,212,000	24.9
1972	696,879	49,129,000	19.1
1973	698,840	50,777,000	17.7
1974	983,504	57,073,000	18.5
1975	1,050,527	55,030,000	16.4
1976	1,208,165	67,887,000	18.9
1977	1,255,265	57,949,000	14.8
1978	1,385,014	60,509,000	13.5
1979	1,482,000	63,046,000	12.8
1980	1,899,300	66,738,000	12.9
1981	2,229,600	70,942,000	12.9
1982	2,447,800	76,591,000	12.9
1983	2,846,900	80,031,000	12.5
1984	2,721,000	92,270,000	12.9
1985	3,242,100	121,057,000	14.8
1986	3,808,600	132,816,000	15.0
1987	4,746,200	152,152,000	15.4
1988	4,719,000	180,583,000	17.7
1989	4,873,200	195,862,000	17.3

(Table continues.)

7

TABLE 1–1 (continued)

Year	Estimated Cost[a] ($)	Franchise Tax Revenues ($)	Franchise Tax as % of Total Tax Collected
1990	6,398,400	200,201,000	17.7
Average			15.5

a. State outlay, for fiscal year ending June 30, on maintenance of corporate chartering business, including appropriations to the division of corporations in the secretary of state's office, courts hearing corporate law cases, and special allocations for corporation code revision (1960, 1961, and 1964).

SOURCES: *Laws of Delaware*, vols. 52–67 (Wilmington: State of Delaware; 1959–1989); U.S. Bureau of the Census, *State Government Tax Collections* (Washington, D.C.: Government Printing Office), various years from 1960 to 1990.

franchise fees in large commercial states are greater than in Delaware, the amount is an infinitesimal proportion of their total tax revenue (table 1–2). These data provide a conservative estimate of the profitability of Delaware's chartering business (table 1–1); revenues are understated by ignoring the increased income taxes paid by state residents who service Delaware corporations, and expenditures are overstated by including the entire state court budget although only a fraction of cases involves corporation law.[15] Delaware's dominance is a stable and persistent phenomenon: it has been the leading incorporation state since the 1920s.

15. Tax revenues are obtained from the U.S. Bureau of the Census, *State Tax Collections*, 1960–1990. Expenditures are obtained from the *Laws of Delaware*, vols. 52–67 (1959–1989), and include all appropriations to the chancery and supreme courts and the division of corporations, which appear after 1972 as a separate item in the state budget. For prior years, expenditures include the entire appropriation to the office of the secretary of state, which administers the division of corporations. To provide a conservative estimate of the profitability of chartering to Delaware as stated in the text, these figures deliberately overestimate the cost to Delaware of administering its chartering business, because only 30 percent of chancery court cases are corporate law cases, "Chancery Court High Stakes in Delaware," *National Law Journal* (February 13, 1984), p. 32, and the proportion of state supreme court cases is undoubtedly lower, and because the ratio of the division of corporations' budget to the budget of the secretary of state office's budget, when the separate figures are available, is only 77 percent.

The dynamic business environment in which firms operate places a premium on a state's responsiveness to corporations' legislative demands, that is, on a state's ability to adapt its corporation code to changing business circumstances. It also places a premium on a decentralized regime: the trial-and-error process of interjurisdictional competition enables a more accurate identification of optimal corporate arrangements when there is fluidity in business conditions. Delaware excels in both dimensions. It has consistently been the most responsive state: if Delaware is not the pioneer for a corporate law innovation, it is among the first to imitate.

The extraordinary success of tiny Delaware in the corporate charter market due to its responsiveness to changing corporate demands is the source, then, of a recurrent corporate law debate on the efficacy of federalism. Who benefits from the laws produced in a federal system, and, in particular, from Delaware's corporation code: managers, who select the state of incorporation, or shareholders, who ratify that selection? Does state competition produce corporation codes that mitigate the agency problem or exacerbate it? If state codes favor managers over shareholders, then from the objective of corporate law itself, the output of state competition is undesirable. Whether the current allocation of authority between the state governments and the national government should be maintained under such circumstances depends on whether the outcome would differ under a national corporation code.

The best assessment of the evidence is that state chartering is for the better and that Delaware's code, for the most part, benefits shareholders. Indeed, the debate's focus in the late 1980s shifted away from Delaware toward the actions of other states, with the widespread enactment of state laws regulating takeovers (corporate acquisitions that take the form of a tender offer to shareholders and thereby, in contrast to mergers, avoid the need for incumbent management's consent). In this important area of statutory innovation, an interesting role reversal occurred: Delaware was a laggard rather than a leader.

Until the Supreme Court upheld state takeover regulation in 1987,[16] takeover statutes could be largely ignored when evaluating the efficacy of state charter competition. The persistent and rapid diffusion of takeover statutes across the states thereafter presented an apparently thorny question for advocates of federalism. Many

---

16. CTS Corp. v. Dynamics Corp. of America, 481 U.S. 69 (1987).

TABLE 1–2
FRANCHISE REVENUE AS A PROPORTION OF TAXES COLLECTED, BY
STATE, 1960–1990
(percent)

State	1960	1970	1980	1990
Alabama	3.1	2.3	2.4	2.7
Alaska	0.4	0.5	0.1	0.1
Arizona	0.5	0.2	0.1	0.1
Arkansas	0.5	0.4	0.3	0.3
California	0.1	0.1	0.02	0.1
Colorado	0.5	0.3	0.2	0.1
Connecticut	0.5	0.2	0.2	0.2
Delaware	13.7	22.5	12.9	17.7
Florida	0.4	0.4	0.2	0.3
Georgia	0.5	0.4	0.3	0.3
Hawaii	0.1	0.1	0.1	0.1
Idaho	0.6	0.5	0.3	0.02
Illinois	0.7	0.9	0.5	0.7
Indiana	0.3	0.1	0.1	0.1
Iowa	0.1	0.1	1.0	0.9
Kansas	0.4	0.3	0.5	0.5
Kentucky	0.8	0.6	0.6	1.8
Louisiana	3.2	3.1	2.8	6.3
Maine	0.5	0.2	0.1	0.2
Maryland	0.2	0.1	0.1	0.1
Massachusetts	NA[a]	0.2	0.1	0.2
Michigan	7.6	5.3	0.1	0.1
Minnesota	0.1	0.1	0.04	0.04
Mississippi	1.8	1.9	2.0	1.8
Missouri	1.9	2.5	1.3	1.2
Montana	0.2	0.1	0.1	0.1
Nebraska	0.6	0.5	0.3	0.3
Nevada	1.1	0.6	0.5	0.4
New Hampshire	0.6	0.9	1.0	0.1
New Jersey	8.7	NA[b]	3.7	1.3

TABLE 1–2 (continued)

State	1960	1970	1980	1990
New Mexico	0.9	0.6	0.6	0.1
New York	0.2	0.1	0.1	0.1
North Carolina	1.8	1.7	1.5	1.7
North Dakota	0.1	0.1	0.1	0.1
Ohio	5.4	6.7	1.7	2.0
Oklahoma	1.2	1.2	1.0	0.9
Oregon	0.3	0.3	0.2	0.2
Pennsylvania	5.4	4.5	3.9	4.6
Rhode Island	0.2	0.3	0.3	0.3
South Carolina	0.4	0.3	0.3	0.6
South Dakota	0.2	0.1	0.1	0.1
Tennessee	2.7	2.6	2.4	4.6
Texas	7.6	5.7	5.2	4.1
Utah	0.2	NA[c]	NA[c]	NA[c]
Vermont	0.1	0.1	0.1	0.1
Virginia	0.4	0.2	0.2	0.3
Washington	0.3	0.2	0.1	0.1
West Virginia	0.5	0.4	0.3	0.2
Wisconsin	0.1	0.1	0.1	0.1
Wyoming	0.4	0.3	0.2	0.3
District of Columbia	NA[d]	NA[d]	0.1	0.2

a. Not available because 1960 franchise tax revenues include corporation net income taxes.
b. Allocation between business franchise and corporation net income not available for 1970.
c. No business franchise tax applicable as of 1970.
d. Not reported.
SOURCE: U.S. Bureau of the Census, *State Government Tax Collections* (Washington, D.C.: Government Printing Office), various years from 1960 to 1990.

commentators consider these statutes harmful to shareholders, as the aim is to thwart takeovers, from which shareholders benefit handsomely while top managers lose out.[17] The question, then, is how

17. For example, Frank H. Easterbrook and Daniel R. Fischel, *The Economic Structure of Corporate Law* (Cambridge: Harvard University Press, 1991), pp. 224–27.

best to understand their enactment. Is there something special about takeover laws compared with other provisions in a corporation code that suggests that they are legislative anomalies? If this is the situation, takeover regulation might merit a jurisdictional exception, to come under exclusive national government control. But if there is no basis for distinguishing the legislative process of takeover statutes or their impact on investors from that of other corporation code provisions, then persistence of takeover statutes could call into question the efficacy of the entire federal system.

The Plan of the Book

This monograph examines the making of American corporate law. After describing the dynamics of the corporate charter market in chapters 2 and 3, it evaluates whether confidence in the efficacy of state competition should be shaken by the recent onslaught of state legislation regulating takeovers. Chapter 4 answers that the saga of state takeover statutes does not support advocates of a national corporation law. While state competition is an imperfect public policy instrument, on balance it benefits investors. There is little basis for supposing that national regulation of corporate charters would be for the better, and there are sound reasons for supposing it would be for the worse. Chapter 5 examines an issue related to state competition for charters, the debate over enabling, as opposed to mandatory, code provisions. It also explores the rationale for and efficacy of federal securities laws and state merit regulation, which are mandatory provisions, and reviews a disturbing trend, from the viewpoint of federalism, the criminalization of fiduciary duties under the federal mail and wire fraud statutes.

To identify more precisely what makes state competition for corporate charters work in the United States, chapter 6 compares the U.S. experience with that of Canada and Europe. Interestingly enough, despite its federal system, Canada has no Delaware. Nor is there a European Delaware. The most convincing explanation for the difference between the United States and Canada concerns the overlapping authority for corporate governance between Canadian provinces and securities commissions, which prevents provinces from asserting exclusive jurisdiction over governance matters and therefore impedes competition for charters. There are several barriers, legal and otherwise, reviewed in chapter 6, that inhibit the development of competition for corporate charters in the European Community. The analysis highlights the importance for facilitating competition of conflict-of-law rules for corporate governance, which differ across common and civil law systems. The chapter also surveys the literature on comparative productivity and concludes that there is no evidence that differences in economic performance are driven by differences in corporate governance arrangements.

The discussion on Canada and the EC is far more speculative than that on the American corporate chartering market, because there has been limited or no empirical research on the political economy of corporate charters in these contexts. Because of pervasive differences in underlying institutional arrangements across nations, the most important being the depth of capital markets and choice-of-law rules, extrapolation and prediction from the U.S. experience to other settings are hazardous endeavors. Despite these limitations, it is possible to draw some tentative and qualified conclusions concerning the Canadian and European corporate law regimes and to gain a deeper appreciation of the merits of the American system.

13

2

The Federalism Debate

THE CLASSIC POSITIONS in the modern debate on whether state corporation codes benefit shareholders were formulated in the 1970s by William Cary, professor at Columbia Law School and former commissioner of the Securities and Exchange Commission, and Ralph Winter, professor at Yale Law School (currently a federal appeals court judge). Cary contended that Delaware's heavy reliance on incorporation fees for revenue led it to engage in a "race for the bottom" with other states to adopt laws that favor managers over shareholders.[1] He therefore advocated national corporate law standards to end state competition. Cary's position was, for many years, the consensus view of commentators on corporate law,[2] and his agenda still attracts support.

A Race for the Bottom or to the Top?

Winter identified a crucial flaw in Cary's analysis, which, when corrected, suggested that the race was more to the top than the bottom: Cary had overlooked the many markets in which firms operate—the capital, product, and corporate control markets—and that constrain managers from choosing a legal regime detrimental to the shareholders' interest.[3] While agreeing with Cary's characteriza-

---

1. William L. Cary, "Federalism and Corporate Law: Reflections upon Delaware," *Yale Law Journal*, vol. 88 (1974), p. 663.

2. In June 1976, for example, eighty law professors signed a letter endorsing a role for the national government in corporate law. See letter submitted by David L. Chambers, in U.S. Congress, Senate, Committee on Commerce, *Hearings on Corporate Rights and Responsibilities*, 94th Congress, 2d session, 1976, p. 343.

3. Ralph K. Winter, "State Law, Shareholder Protection, and the Theory of the Corporation," *Journal of Legal Studies*, vol. 6 (1977), p. 251; Ralph K. Winter,

tion of the power of competition in producing laws that firms demand, Winter's important point was that firms operating under a legal regime that did not maximize firm value would be outperformed by firms operating under a legal regime that did and the former would therefore have lower stock prices. A lower stock price could subject a firm's managers to either employment termination, as the firm is driven out of business because of a higher cost of capital than that of competitors operating under a value-maximizing regime, or replacement by a successful takeover bidder that could increase a firm's value by reincorporating (the term of art for a change in statutory domicile). Winter concluded that this threat of job displacement would lead managers to demand a value-maximizing regime for their shareholders and that states would provide it, as such a strategy maintains, if not enhances, a state's incorporation business. Winter's critique forced adherents of the Cary position to amend it. The contention became that markets are imperfect constraints on managers and, hence, there is sufficient slack in the system to produce non–value-maximizing state laws.

In both the Cary and the Winter positions, the goal of maximizing revenues functions as an invisible hand guiding the decentralized system of state corporation laws to codify the arrangements that firms desire. The crux of their disagreement concerns whose demand schedule for corporate charters is driving the system. Cary and the proponents of a national corporation code consider the demand function to be derived from managers' preferences. They view the state legislative process as a political market failure in which managers are better organized than the more numerous but dispersed shareholders, and they characterize managers' preferences for codes as diametrically opposed to those of shareholders'. Winter and advocates of state chartering conclude that shareholders' preferences determine firms' demand because of the constraining influence on managers of the many markets in which firms operate, which reduces or eliminates the agency problem. They further maintain that even if there is slack in the system (there is, as shown in subsequent chapters), it does not follow that national legislation would do a better job than state competition at mitigating the agency problem. Of

---

Government and the Corporation (Washington, D.C.: American Enterprise Institute, 1978).

15

course, in the absence of conflict between shareholder and manager preferences, the debate is moot, since the substantive content of state laws would be invariant with whoever, managers or shareholders, makes the incorporation decision or lobbies state legislators. The choice of incorporation state would therefore automatically enhance the value of the firm and, accordingly, shareholder wealth.

While the revenue-maximization explanation of state chartering—to which both sides of the debate subscribe—is intuitively compelling to those familiar with the field, a natural empirical question is whether there is interjurisdictional competition for corporate charters. The evidence supports the view that states do compete for the chartering business. Innovations in corporation codes that firms emphasize as provisions leading them to change their incorporation state spread rapidly across the states in a pattern resembling the S-shaped diffusion curve of technological innovations.[4] In addition, when corporate migration patterns are examined, we find that states that are more responsive to firms' desires gain more and lose fewer corporations than less responsive states.[5] Finally, there is a significant positive correlation between the responsiveness of a state's corporation code and the proportion of state revenues derived from incorporation (franchise) taxes.[6] The most responsive state, Delaware, often pioneers new code provisions, but this is not always the case; it excels because when it is not the first to innovate, it is among the first to imitate.

Since the publication of the Cary and Winter articles, empirical studies have sought to arbitrate the debate over who benefits from state competition, shareholders or managers, by measuring the economic impact of managerial discretion to choose among alternative corporation codes by changing a firm's state of incorporation. They conclude that the choice benefits rather than harms shareholders.

---

4. Roberta Romano, "Law as a Product: Some Pieces of the Incorporation Puzzle," *Journal of Law, Economics, and Organization*, vol. 1 (1985), p. 225.

5. To measure a state's responsiveness, an index was constructed as a linear function of the year of enactment of four specific corporate law reforms that are identified by reincorporating firms as a reason for their new domicile choice; ibid., pp. 237–38.

6. Ibid. The statistical relation holds, even when the Delaware observations are eliminated.

The conclusion rests on widely accepted financial econometric techniques known as event studies, which examine whether particular information events (discrete public events introducing new information to financial markets), such as a firm's decision to change its state of incorporation, significantly affect a firm's stock price (technically, they examine whether the average residuals of a regression of observed stock prices on predicted prices are statistically significantly different from zero). If an information event—in this instance, reincorporating in Delaware—is considered beneficial for shareholders (that is, if it enhances the value of their equity investment), then stock prices will rise significantly above their expected value on the public announcement of the event. If the event is perceived as detrimental to shareholder wealth, then stock prices will significantly decline. Given the regression methodology, such stock price effects are referred to as average residuals or abnormal returns. The posited relationships between changes in stock price and reincorporation announcements restate the Winter and Cary theses in testable form: Cary's thesis that shareholders are harmed by Delaware's code implies that firms should experience a significant negative price effect when they announce a reincorporation in Delaware. Similarly, Winter's hypothesis predicts a positive effect.

There have been five event studies of reincorporation[7] (summa-

---

7. Peter Dodd and Richard Leftwich, "The Market for Corporate Charters: 'Unhealthy Competition' vs. Federal Regulation," *Journal of Business*, vol. 53 (1980), p. 259; Allen Hyman, "The Delaware Controversy—The Legal Debate," *Journal of Corporate Law*, vol. 4 (1979), p. 368; Romano, "Law as a Product"; Michael Bradley and Cindy A. Schipani, "The Relevance of the Duty of Care Standard in Corporate Governance," *Iowa Law Review*, vol. 75 (1989), p. 1; Jeffry Netter and Annette Poulsen, "State Corporation Laws and Shareholders: The Recent Experience," *Financial Management*, vol. 18 (1989), p. 29. In an otherwise excellent textbook, William Klein and John Coffee incorrectly report the literature's findings when they state that "stock price studies have shown little or no change in share prices when a corporation moves from one jurisdiction to another" and that there is a "significant gain" when firms "reincorporate in Delaware to take advantage of its antitakeover rules"; William A. Klein and John C. Coffee, *Business Organizations and Finance*, 5th ed. (Westbury, N.Y.: Foundation Press, 1993), pp. 145–46 n. 34. Firms reincorporating in aggregate experienced a significant positive abnormal return of 4 percent, an increase that would be impressive to any portfolio manager; firms reincorporating to undertake acquisitions experienced significant gains whereas those reincorporating for antitakeover reasons experienced insignificant positive returns; Romano, "Law as a Product," p. 271.

rized in table 2–1). While several have found significant positive stock price effects on firms' reincorporation to Delaware, *no* study has found a negative stock price effect as Cary would predict. The data are most consistent with Winter's hypothesis of the efficacy of competition.

Some advocates of national corporation laws question the usefulness of event studies. Lucian Bebchuk and Melvin Eisenberg contend that event studies do not indicate investors' evaluation of the new state's regime because of possibly confounding signals: if a reincorporation announcement is accompanied by disclosure of a new corporate strategy, a positive stock price reaction may be due to investors' assessment of the new strategy and not of the value of the new statutory domicile.[8] It is, however, improbable that such information could swamp a reincorporation's otherwise significantly negative stock price effect. If this hypothesis of an offsetting effect is correct and reincorporation is a wealth-decreasing event, we should observe a significant negative stock price for firms changing domicile to engage in activities that are perceived as favoring managers over shareholders—and not for those firms reincorporating to undertake activities that are deemed beneficial to shareholders. This is because in the former case, there would be no such offsetting effect. The stock price effect is not, however, significantly different across firms reincorporating for different business purposes, that is, for those planning to undertake activities that commentators consider adverse to shareholders' interest (fortifying takeover defensive tactics) and those that they do not criticize (implementing a program of mergers and acquisitions or reducing taxes).[9] Moreover, shareholders must approve a reincorporation, and the SEC requires detailed disclosure of differences in legal regimes in proxy materials. Informed share-

---

8. Lucian A. Bebchuk, "Federalism and the Corporation: The Desirable Limits on State Competition in Corporate Law," *Harvard Law Review*, vol. 105 (1992), p. 1435; Melvin A. Eisenberg, "The Structure of Corporation Law," *Columbia Law Review*, vol. 89 (1989), pp. 1461, 1508; see also Romano, "Law as a Product." Firms often disclose information concerning corporate policy changes at the time of a reincorporation, undertaking the move to reduce the cost of the new strategy's implementation. See Romano, "Law as a Product."

9. Romano, "Law as a Product," p. 272. The reasons why commentators view antitakeover defenses negatively from the shareholders' perspective are reviewed in chapter 4.

holders will not approve a move to a destination state whose regime is adverse to their interest. If to coerce approval of a non–value-maximizing domicile, management threatened not to undertake a newly proposed value-maximizing strategy for the firm should shareholders not approve reincorporation, such conduct would be a breach of fiduciary duty.[10]

Bebchuk further questions whether event studies can ever resolve the debate on state competition. He asserts that even if the current conclusions of positive or insignificant stock price effects on reincorporation are bolstered by further studies finding even stronger positive effects, this will not arbitrate the Cary-Winter debate, because there could always be some code provision that disadvantages shareholders but whose negative impact is netted out by greater positive price effects of other code provisions. Bebchuk's contention, while cast as a criticism of the empirical basis for supporting a federal system of state corporation laws, actually acknowledges that state competition is on the whole beneficial for shareholders, for the effect of good provisions outweighs the bad. Far from shifting the burden of proof from advocates of national regulation to advocates of state competition, the argument implies that because state competition generally benefits shareholders, those who would promote Cary's position have the burden of demonstrating empirically which particular code provisions harm shareholders and why national legislation would be more likely to alleviate the problem.

Ancillary evidence on the effect of state competition comes from a more contemporary example of the diffusion of an important corporation code innovation, the late-1980s statutory reform permitting firms to limit directors' personal liability for damages in shareholder suits. In this instance, Delaware was a pioneering state; within two years of Delaware's innovation, forty-one states had similar statutes.[11] If Cary's claim is accurate and the states are in a race for the bottom, then we ought to observe negative stock returns both for firms reincorporating to Delaware to take advantage of the limited liability statute and for Delaware firms on the statute's enactment. Firms changing statutory domicile to take advantage of Delaware's

---

10. See Lacos Land Co. v. Arden Group, 517 A.2d 271 (Del.Ch. 1986).

11. Roberta Romano, "Corporate Governance in the Aftermath of the Insurance Crisis," *Emory Law Journal*, vol. 39 (1990), p. 1155.

TABLE 2–1
EVENT STUDIES BEARING ON STATE COMPETITION

Study	Effect on Stock Prices
Reincorporation	
Hyman (1979)	Positive returns 4 days before event
Dodd and Leftwich (1980)	Positive CARs 2 years before event[a]
Romano (1985)	Positive CARs at 3-, 5-, 21-day intervals around event, for aggregate and subportfolios for mergers and miscellaneous reincorporations[a]
Bradley and Schipani (1989)	Positive AR on event date[a]
Netter and Poulsen (1989)	Positive CARs 1 month around event[b]
Delaware Limited Liability Statute	
Bradley and Schipani (1989)	Negative AR on effective date[a]
Janjigian and Bolster (1990)	Negative AR on newspaper announcement day and day of introduction to senate[a]
Romano (1990)	Negative AR on effective date, day after newspaper report, and day after senate action[a]
Firms Adopting Limited Liability Charter Provisions	
Bradley and Schipani (1989)	Negative CARs at 7-day interval around event[a]
Netter and Poulsen (1989)	No effect
Janjigian and Bolster (1990)	No effect
Romano (1990)	Positive CARs at 2-, 3-, and 5-day intervals around event;[a] no effect at 7-day interval

NOTES: AR = average residual or abnormal return, the difference between observed and predicted stock prices on the event date, estimated by an ordinary least squares regression based on the market model, $AR = R - (\alpha + \beta R_m)$, where R_m is the return on the market portfolio, R the return on the stock, and the parameters α and β are estimated over a lengthy interval before the event date; CAR = average residuals cumulated over an event interval.
a. Significant at 5 percent or less.
b. Significant at 10 percent.

(Table notes continue.)

20

new statute experienced either significant positive abnormal returns or positive abnormal returns bordering on conventional statistical significance (10 percent). [12]

The incremental effect of the statute can be determined for firms already incorporated in Delaware through an event study examining the stock price effect of charter amendments limiting director liability, because the statute required that firms opt in to be covered. As indicated in table 2–1, the results are suggestive but not conclusive: one study finds a significant positive stock price effect, two find an insignificantly positive effect, and one finds a significant negative effect. [13] Because the sign of the price effect in the majority of studies

---

12. Bradley and Schipani, "Relevance of the Duty of Care Standard"; Netter and Poulsen, "State Corporation Laws and Shareholders." The findings of these studies are summarized in table 2–1 with those of the general reincorporation event studies.

13. I found a significant positive effect over the intervals closest to the event: days 0 to +1, −1 to +1, −2 to +2, and an insignificant positive effect over the longer interval, −3 to +3, as well as over the 71-day period day −10 to +60. Romano, "Corporate Governance," p. 1184. The latter result is consistent with the findings of two studies that the amendments produced no significant stock price effect. Netter and Poulsen, "State Corporation Laws and Shareholders"; Vahan Janjigian and Paul J. Bolster, "The Elimination of Director Liability and Stockholder Returns: An Empirical Investigation," *Journal of Financial Research*, vol. 13 (1990), p. 53. Bradley and Schipani, "Relevance of the Duty of Care Standard," report significantly negative abnormal returns over days −3 to +3 and do not report results for any other event interval. The limited reporting of results suggests that Bradley and Schipani did not find negative returns over any other interval, and, indeed, they report insignificant positive residuals for 10 days after the event. To explore the

---

(Table 2–1 continued.)
SOURCES: Allen Hyman, "The Delaware Controversy—The Legal Debate," *Journal of Corporate Law*, vol. 4 (1979); Peter Dodd and Richard Leftwich, "The Market for Corporate Charters: 'Unhealthy Competition' vs. Federal Regulation," *Journal of Business*, vol. 53 (1980); Roberta Romano, "Law as a Product: Some Pieces of the Incorporation Puzzle," *Journal of Law, Economics, and Organization*, vol. 1 (1985); Michael Bradley and Cindy A. Schipani, "The Relevance of the Duty of Care Standard in Corporate Governance," *Iowa Law Review*, vol. 75 (1989); Jeffrey Netter and Annette Poulsen, "State Corporation Laws and Shareholders: The Recent Experience," *Financial Management*, vol. 18 (1989); Vahan Janijhigian and Paul J. Bolster, "The Elimination of Director Liability and Stockholder Returns: An Empirical Investigation," *Journal of Financial Research*, vol. 13 (1990); and Roberta Romano, "Corporate Governance in the Aftermath of the Insurance Crisis," *Emory Law Journal*, vol. 39 (1990).

is positive and the negative effect occurs over a less precise event interval than the positive one (the interval around the event is longer, and therefore the dating of the release of the information to the public is less accurate), the more plausible conclusion is that shareholders evaluate coverage under a limited liability statute positively or with indifference rather than negatively. This is consistent with studies of shareholder litigation that find that the lawsuits eliminated by these amendments (duty of care cases) rarely produce significant recoveries for shareholders.[14]

Event studies of charter amendments may not, however, accurately identify an amendment's effect if investors anticipate that firms will adopt conforming charter amendments when the enabling statute is enacted. Under this scenario, the effect of limited liability charter amendments will have been impounded into stock prices at the earlier time of the statute's enactment, and an event study of the amendments should not find significant stock price effects. This hypothesis (no effect on amendment because of rational expectations; that is, shareholders correctly anticipate the forthcoming action) is consistent with the findings of two of the four event studies of firms adopting limited liability charter provisions. An event study of the legislative process is therefore required to determine the effect on stock prices of the statute and hence of such amendments. Evaluating the stock price effect of legislation is, however, more complicated than an event study of a firm-specific occurrence, such as charter amendments or reincorporations, because a lengthy legislative process makes identification of the information event difficult and the

---

difference in our studies, I plotted the cumulative abnormal returns in relation to a confidence interval of two standard deviations for a longer period of -10 to $+60$ days around the event, and the CARs were significantly positive for approximately half of the 71-day period, and insignificant for the rest of the period. The studies' samples and parameter estimation period differ, which may account for the difference: I use the standard technique of estimating the parameters through day -11 while they use an earlier period ending at day -40, and they find significant negative returns over the period -40 to -1. This suggests that their expected returns in the event period will look worse compared with the benchmark returns than mine. It is unlikely that anticipated knowledge of the proxy proposal explains the lower returns in the beginning of Bradley and Schipani's estimation period, and hence they appear not to be accurately estimating the limited liability amendment's effect, compared with my study.

14. See Romano, "Corporate Governance," pp. 1168–71.

power of the statistical test in event studies depends on accurately identifying the event date. If the event date is imprecisely specified, significance tests for the average residuals will be improperly calibrated—for instance, the null hypothesis of no significance may be rejected more frequently than is appropriate—especially when the event's date is the same calendar date for all firms, as with legislation, as opposed to charter amendments or reincorporations.[15]

As summarized in table 2–1, several event studies have sought to isolate the impact of Delaware's limited liability statute.[16] Delaware firms experienced insignificant negative abnormal returns during the event interval covering the legislative process, from introduction to enactment of the limited liability statute. The stock price effect is significantly negative on the statute's effective date. Although one study fixes on this result in evaluating the statute's impact on shareholder wealth, this finding is, in fact, irrelevant to such an assessment, because no new information concerning the legislation, such as the likelihood of enactment, was released on the effective date, which was twelve days after the statute's enactment. The effective date of a statute is an empty formality, not an information event, when it is not the same date as the statute's enactment. Hence we cannot attribute a stock price reaction on such a date to investors' evaluation of the legislation.

On two other dates before the effective date, depending on the study, an interval surrounding senate action and press reports of the enactment of the limited liability statute, the average residuals are also significantly negative. But the average residuals cumulated over all the legislative events (either over the event dates only or intervals around the dates as well)—which are termed cumulative average residuals (CARs)—are not significant. If the statute adversely affected shareholders, there should be a sustained negative effect over the cumulated legislative events.[17] Moreover, the CARs of Delaware

---

15. This result is shown in a comprehensive examination of the properties of the statistical tests in event studies by Stephen J. Brown and Jerold B. Warner, "Using Daily Stock Returns: The Case of Event Studies," *Journal of Financial Economics*, vol. 14 (1985), pp. 3, 15.

16. Bradley and Schipani, "Relevance of the Duty of Care Standard"; Janjigian and Bolster, "Elimination of Director Liability"; Netter and Poulsen, "State Corporation Laws and Shareholders"; Romano, "Corporate Governance."

17. Such results are found in event studies of other statutes involving takeover

firms are not significantly different from the CARs of non-Delaware firms over the event interval.[18] The most cogent interpretation of these data, as three of the four event studies conclude, is that the limited liability statute did not adversely affect shareholders, a conclusion more consistent with Winter's than Cary's characterization of state competition.

State Competition for Close Corporations

The discussion so far has focused on concerns of large public corporations, for which event studies analyzing stock price effects can aid in evaluating the efficacy of state competition. Most businesses, however, begin their corporate existence as close corporations, for which there is no stock market to signal the efficacy of particular code provisions. The key protection of the capital market that Winter emphasizes as ensuring the efficacy of state competition is thus of little relevance to closely held firms. The agency problem underlying code provisions for public corporations is also less severe in the close corporation setting because ownership and control are typically not severed. Concerns of close corporation shareholders involve instead conflicts between majority and minority shareholders and between shareholder-managers and nonmanaging shareholders, as well as valuation problems for shareholders that arise from the absence of a public market for shares. Given these contrasting concerns, it is not surprising that many states have enacted special close corporation statutes. But the disparate circumstances of public and close corporations also raise the questions whether states compete for close corporation charters and, accordingly, whether the product benefits close corporation shareholders.

Ian Ayres contends that states do not compete for close corporation charters, because the revenues that are obtained from luring such firms' incorporations are meager.[19] As Ayres details it, under

---

regulation, which are discussed in chapter 4, for example, Greg Sidak and Susan Woodward, "Corporate Takeovers, the Commerce Clause, and the Efficient Anonymity of Shareholders," *Northwestern Law Review*, vol. 84 (1990), p. 1092 (significant negative CARs for legislative history of Indiana takeover statute).

18. Janjigian and Bolster, "Elimination of Director Liability," pp. 57–59.

19. Ian Ayres, "Judging Close Corporations in the Age of Statutes," *Washington University Law Quarterly*, vol. 70 (1992), p. 365.

Delaware's fee structure, for example, a typical close corporation would pay an annual franchise tax of $50 compared with more than $100,000 in tax paid by a larger public firm.[20] Thus, by Ayres's calculation, even if all small businesses were incorporated in Delaware, its current level of franchise tax revenue would not double.[21] Delaware's attentiveness, however, is not simply a function of franchise tax revenues; the state benefits from the increase in income earned by its citizens—attorneys and other residents—who service Delaware corporations. Nevertheless, Ayres makes an important point: if the relative profitability of servicing close corporations is much less than that of public corporations, the ancillary benefits produced by competing for close corporation charters would in all likelihood also be small. Moreover, it is more costly for close corporations to reincorporate in Delaware than for public ones, as the former will bear an additional layer of tax that the typical public firm doing business in numerous states must pay anyway. Because there are consequently fewer marginal buyers of close corporate charters than of public ones, competitive pressures on legislatures to supply an adequate product are reduced.

Even if states do not have the high-powered incentives of tax revenues to compete for the chartering business of close corporations, they may still have an incentive to produce efficacious close corporation codes: there may be spillover effects for their public corporation business, such as developing a reputation of having a good business climate. Accordingly, rather than rely on estimates of potential revenue, further research correlating responsiveness to concerns of close corporations with responsiveness to those of public corporations—such as examining whether the innovators in general corporate law reform like Delaware are also the first states to adopt close corporation statutes—is necessary to evaluate Ayres's claim better.

Ayres does not contend that shareholders of close corporations are necessarily harmed by state codes in the absence of competition. Rather, he asserts that, given the lack of financial incentives, state legislatures will not be responsive to the needs of close corporations and, as a consequence, courts will play a larger role in fashioning

---

20. Ibid., p. 377.

21. Ibid., p. 378 (calculating a maximum increase of $150 million over current revenues of $200 million).

the law of close corporations than legislatures. There have been several examples, supporting his view, of judicial nullification of corporation statutes in the close corporation setting, typically to permit greater contracting flexibility to the parties than a code that focused on public corporation needs appeared to allow.[22] In these instances, legislatures thereafter amended the statutes to codify judicial opinions.

But there is a plausible explanation besides Ayres's explanation of legislative indifference for a larger judicial role in corporate law innovation for close corporations than for public corporations.[23] It is likely that standard form contracts are less useful for parties in closely held businesses than public corporations, because there is far greater diversity in ownership, management, and control arrangements in such firms. Such a difference would account for an expanded judicial role in the close corporation context. For if there are no obvious default rules, then there is not much benefit from state competition for close corporation charters, nor would private parties place much of a premium on it.

Partnership statutes provide a helpful analogy. There does not appear to be a preferred domicile for partnerships. Rather, all states have adopted a version of a uniform statute, the Uniform Partnership Act. The UPA is an enabling statute concerning intrapartnership affairs: it provides defaults where a partnership agreement is silent. Because the particulars of partnerships are so varied—the organizational form covers a diverse and eclectic set of businesses—parties' counsel generally draft explicit partnership agreements rather than rely on the UPA defaults, and courts, as contract interpreters, are therefore more important than legislatures for the participants in such businesses.

A standard form contract is appropriate for corporations that experience common, recurring problems, because, although corporation codes permit customizing, they are most valuable when firms can opt for their defaults, as this reduces information costs (firms do not have to draft their own charters, and investors do not have to

---

22. For examples, see ibid.

23. This contention is developed in Roberta Romano, "State Competition for Close Corporation Charters: A Commentary," *Washington University Law Quarterly*, vol. 70 (1992), p. 409.

investigate firm charters before purchasing stock). Public corporation charters, for example, tend to be clean documents—short and uncluttered, with little detail beyond statutory requirements—with particulars left for corporate bylaws, which are easier to revise as business conditions change. When business relations are relatively specialized and idiosyncratic, as in the context of close corporations, which are often characterized as incorporated partnerships, disputes among investors will not turn on interpretation of standard default rules, and courts become crucial players, given their superior ability compared with legislatures to arbitrate particularized disputes. Namely, unlike legislatures, courts are set up to answer questions that do not arise in time to be resolved before the dispute. (They are ex post, not ex ante, decision makers).[24]

Furthermore, quite apart from having fewer resources to expend on lobbying state legislatures, many close corporation disputes occur in endgame settings (the parties will not be continuing in a long-term relation of repeated play), where there will be no gains from future relations. This alters the cost-benefit calculation of legislative lobbying compared with seeking a personal ruling from a court. In an endgame, there is scant benefit from the costs of lobbying for a statutory change: it will be used only once in the parties' mutual dealings, because the relationship is terminating. The cost-benefit calculation of approaching a legislature for close corporations is therefore different from that for public corporations, whose contractual disputes often recur, as their transactions are far more numerous and they are longer-lived.

The difference in cost-effective legal strategies for close and public corporations is important because of a common feature of legislatures. Legislators tend to function more analogously to firemen than police: they need to be notified by constituents that something is wrong (constituents pull a fire alarm) to take action, as their busy schedules make them unable to engage in neighborhood patrolling to spot a problem.[25] Since close corporations are unlikely to find it cost-

---

24. Easterbrook and Fischel, *Economic Structure of Corporate Law*, p. 35.

25. The analogy is from Mathew D. McCubbins and Thomas Schwartz, "Congressional Oversight Overlooked: Police Patrols versus Fire Alarms," *American Journal of Political Science*, vol. 28 (1984), p. 165, who argue that the more efficient approach for Congress to oversight of administrative agencies is the fire alarm rather than police patrol approach.

effective to seek legislative relief, when courts invalidate or radically reinterpret statutes constraining close corporations they are not competing with the legislature or usurping the legislative function, as Ayres suggests, but rather they are effectuating and perfecting a legislature's will in a situation where the legislature is not informed of a constituent's difficulty. The contention is that had legislators been informed of the problem, the corporation code would have been amended, eliminating the need for judicial action. This claim is bolstered by the pattern, detailed by Ayres, of state legislatures consistently codifying rather than reversing judicial opinions that nullify corporation code provisions in order to resolve a close corporation dispute.

The Corporate Bar and State Competition

The question whether the potential revenue from producing close corporation charters is significant enough to spark state competition highlights a fundamental premise of both sides of the corporate federalism debate, which merits closer examination: Why would individual legislators want to maximize franchise revenues in the first place? What's in it for them? Two persuasive reasons explain such behavior by legislators. First, higher franchise tax revenues can be used to lower taxes on, or increase services for, in-state constituents. Second, at least one well-organized in-state interest group lobbies the legislature for corporate codes that firms desire because their wealth is implicated as well: the corporate bar.

Lawyers' intimate involvement in the creation of corporation codes raises an additional agency problem for the federalism debate: are lawyers' interests regarding the content of corporation codes aligned with those of shareholders? Jonathan Macey and Geoffrey Miller maintain that there is a significant agency problem between attorneys and corporations and their shareholders and that Delaware's regime exemplifies this problem because it enhances the value of its lawyers' services by increasing the likelihood of litigation.[26] Macey and Miller provide examples of how Delaware's code is more conducive to litigation than other state codes, such as its lack of a security-

---

26. See Jonathan R. Macey and Geoffrey P. Miller, "Toward an Interest-Group Theory of Delaware Corporate Law," *Texas Law Review*, vol. 65 (1987), p. 469.

for-expenses provision requiring suing shareholders to post a bond for defense costs. They do not, however, demonstrate that there is, in fact, an agency problem; that is, that shareholders are harmed by such provisions. In addition, Macey and Miller focus on code provisions encouraging litigation, but several rules decrease the likelihood of lawsuits, such as the demand requirement, which, by requiring a shareholder to make a demand on the board before he can file suit, puts the decision to sue in the board's hands. If, on receiving such a demand, the board determines that the cost of the lawsuit outweighs the potential benefit, it can refuse to litigate and, on the basis of its cost-benefit calculation, successfully obtain dismissal of a lawsuit thereafter filed by the shareholder. Indeed, Delaware has gone further than other states in strictly enforcing the demand requirement.[27]

While the posture of Delaware's code toward shareholder suits is more ambiguous than Macey and Miller suggest, studies attempting to measure the benefits of shareholder litigation somewhat support their conjecture. Consistent with an agency problem, studies fail to uncover much benefit from litigation to shareholders in contrast to their attorneys.[28] This finding, however, holds across all courts, both state and federal, and hence appears unrelated to state competition and, in particular, to the claim that Delaware is more favorable to lawyers than other jurisdictions. Successful attorneys earn higher fees in Delaware compared with other state courts but not compared with federal courts: in a sample of 139 shareholder suits, with 24 cases brought solely in the Delaware Chancery Court, 20 cases solely in other state courts, and 70 in federal court, the average fee awarded in settled cases (1988 dollars) in Delaware is (11 cases) $337,000, compared with $116,000 in other state courts (11 cases) and $1,487,000 in federal court (34 cases).[29] It is difficult to ascertain whether this finding bolsters Macey and Miller's contention concern-

---

27. For example, Levine v. Smith, 591 A.2d 194 (Del. Supr. 1991).

28. For example, Roberta Romano, "The Shareholder Suit: Litigation without Foundation," *Journal of Law, Economics and Organization*, vol. 7 (1991), p. 55 (sample of state and federal cases); Janet Cooper Alexander, "Do the Merits Matter? A Study of Settlements in Securities Class Actions," *Stanford Law Review*, vol. 43 (1991), p. 497 (sample of federal cases).

29. For a description of the sample, see Romano, "The Shareholder Suit."

ing Delaware, because the cases are not scaled for legal complexity or for legal merit, and attorneys' fees are a function of such case characteristics. Given the large size of Delaware corporations (approximately half of the Fortune 500 firms) and the coverage of larger firms under the securities laws (although antifraud provisions of the federal securities laws apply to all corporations, the registration requirements apply only to publicly traded firms or firms with assets greater than $5 million), disparate complexity of litigation is undoubtedly at work.

Although I am skeptical of the strong form of Macey and Miller's claim that Delaware's corporation code favors lawyers over shareholders, Delaware's commanding position in the charter market may possibly enable the corporate bar to siphon a share of Delaware's monopoly rents by generating some laws that decrease firm value and increase attorney income. The trade-off will not reach the point at which a firm will be indifferent between staying put and switching to Delaware. In most situations, however, what increases the value of a firm also increases corporate counsel's wealth, as an impoverished firm will not create much work for corporate law practitioners, and bankruptcy, a specialized practice, entails federal and not state law proceedings.[30] Moreover, a competitive market for lawyers reduces counsels' ability to use Delaware's corporation code to increase litigation so as to benefit themselves at the shareholders' expense. But a firm's counsel has a first-mover advantage that makes it expensive to switch lawyers midstream: that is, attorneys develop expertise about their clients that enables them to provide legal services more cheaply than competitors. This permits attorneys to earn rents, possibly by enacting a legal code that favors counsel, up to the differential value between their services and the market rate. No one, however, has attempted to estimate the extent of such an economic advantage, and casual empiricism suggests that it is not great: for instance, in-house counsel often put work out to bid and use multiple law firms. In addition, a recent study of the legal profession, though not fine-tuned to corporate practice, finds that

---

30. For an argument that state competition would be beneficial in the bankruptcy context, see David Skeel, "Rethinking the Line between Corporate Law and Corporate Bankruptcy" (unpublished manuscript, Temple University, 1993).

lawyers do not make abnormal returns when income is adjusted to years of education.[31]

Legislators, in sum, do have an incentive to be responsive in making corporation codes, even though few shareholders actually vote in local elections. There may well be episodic support for Macey and Miller's thesis, as the empirical studies of shareholder suits suggest that litigation benefits attorneys far more than investors, but it is unlikely that lawyers' interests dictate the comprehensive structure of corporation codes in contrast to those of shareholders, because the problematic features of shareholder litigation afflict lawsuits under federal statutes as well.

---

31. Sherwin Rosen, "The Market for Lawyers," *Journal of Law and Economics*, vol. 35 (1992), p. 215.

3

The Structure of the Corporate Charter Market

WHILE THERE IS CONSENSUS across participants in the state competition debate on states' incentives to obtain franchise fees from public corporations, neither Cary nor Winter offered an explanation of how Delaware is able to maintain its commanding position. The key to Delaware's sustained market share over time involves the marginal consumers in the charter market, reincorporating firms. Their requirements are twofold. First, they seek a legal regime that reduces their cost of doing business. Second, they seek a guarantee that the domicile state will maintain, and not welch on, the desirability of its code. As this chapter reports, Delaware offers a legal regime that is favorable in both dimensions. In explaining Delaware's success, chapter 3 also indicates why Congress cannot duplicate Delaware's role and identifies the genius of American corporate law.

Why Change Statutory Domicile?

The vast majority of firms changing their statutory domicile select one destination, Delaware.[1] But not all firms reincorporate. Firms change their statutory domicile when they expect to engage in business transactions that can be undertaken more cheaply under a new legal regime. A legal regime can directly reduce a transaction's costs (for example, rules governing specific transactions such as voting requirements for acquisitions differ across the states and thereby impose differential costs on such transactions), or it can influence the cost of a transaction more indirectly (for instance, legal

---

1. Romano, "Law as a Product," p. 244 (more than 80 percent of reincorporating firms migrated to Delaware).

regimes differentially affect the likelihood of litigation).

Reincorporating firms typically plan to undertake one of three types of transactions in the immediate future: a public offering of stock (typically the firm's initial public offering), a mergers and acquisitions program, and antitakeover defensive tactics.[2] Such transactions increase the likelihood of a firm being sued. Mergers and acquisitions and defensive maneuvers against takeovers are fraught with the potential for shareholder suits, involving disputes over the fairness of offers or the appropriateness of management's actions.[3] Going public creates a new class of noncontrolling public investors, subjecting insiders to fiduciary suits for conflicts of interest. The change in capital structure to a publicly traded entity increases the importance of the legal regime, because flexibility in the use of informal decision-making procedures, which differ across state codes, is more important when shareholdings are dispersed than when they are closely held. In addition, legal rules on shareholder voting and appraisal rights in acquisitions, which affect the cost of engaging in acquisitions or defensive tactics, vary across states. While innovations in corporate law that are of interest to reincorporating firms are eventually adopted by most states, some firms in laggard states will not wait until their state acts: these footloose firms are the marginal consumers in the corporate charter market.

When management expects a change in corporate activities that increases the probability of shareholder litigation, specific characteristics of the legal regime become important, such as a comprehensive, well-developed case law, which facilitates the ready availability of legal opinions on specific transactions, and clearly specified indemnification rules:[4] such a regime provides greater predictability for structuring transactions and reduces the firm's cost of doing

---

2. Ibid. These three transactions accounted for 72 percent of the reincorporations in a sample of more than 500 public corporations changing statutory domicile between 1960 and 1982.

3. See, for example, Romano, "The Shareholder Suit."

4. These factors are repeatedly mentioned by reincorporating firms as the advantages offered by the destination state. See Romano, "Law as a Product," pp. 250–51.

business. Nearly all migrating firms move from less to more responsive legal regimes.[5] Moreover, firms reincorporating to go public or engage in mergers and acquisitions programs move, in overwhelming numbers, to Delaware, whose code is favorable for undertaking such transactions.[6] Reincorporating firms clearly perceive differences in legal regimes: firms migrating to Delaware considered the difference between old and new legal regimes as substantial and the new regime as an important factor in the decision to move, both more frequently than firms moving to other states.[7]

Reincorporating to obtain more desirable rules is not without a cost. Delaware's franchise tax rate is higher than that of many states, and a firm with no other business in Delaware incurs an additional layer of franchise taxes.[8] In addition, there are one-time costs associated with a domicile move, such as legal fees; the expenses of a shareholder meeting, including printing and postage costs for proxy materials; and state filing fees, to qualify the newly incorporated firm and withdraw the old firm, in the states in which it does business.[9] Moreover, if the firm is not traded on a national exchange (as is true for the firms reincorporating in preparation for their initial public offering), in a number of states there is a further potential cost, which can be substantial: because reincorporation is achieved by merger into a subsidiary shell company incorporated in the new domicile, shareholders can vote against the merger, exercise appraisal rights, and obtain the cash value of their shares when the firm is not traded on a national exchange, draining cash out of the corporation.[10] Because of these costs, few firms reincorporate more than once (less than 5 percent of a sample of more than 500 firms that reincorporated from 1960 to 1982 did so).[11] For a firm to be willing to incur such

---

5. Ibid., pp. 225, 259–60. This responsiveness measure is explained in note 5 of chapter 2.

6. Ibid., pp. 246–47.

7. Ibid., pp. 258–59.

8. Ibid., pp. 255, 257.

9. Ibid., pp. 246–48.

10. I would like to thank Frank Wozencraft for informing me of this reincorporation expense.

11. Romano, "Law as a Product." Bernard Black contends that reincorporation costs are trivial; Black, "Is Corporate Law Trivial? A Political and Economic

expenses and, indeed, to pay a premium for a corporation code, it needs some assurance from the destination state that it will maintain the favorable features of its code should business conditions change.

Analysis," *Northwestern University Law Review*, vol. 84 (1990), p. 542. As the text indicates, the contention is wrong. Besides understating some of the large one-time reincorporation costs described in the text, Black excludes from his calculation the increased costs that firms bear over their lifetime from a move, such as increased listing, tax, and attorney's fees. Such an omission is incorrect. The mistake in Black's analysis is that he has overlooked the economic concept of opportunity costs. As one economics text puts it, "The cost of any chosen act is the most valuable forsaken alternative opportunity. Thus the cost of production of one more unit of butter is the number of guns that otherwise could have been produced. . . . The money spent measures only part of the costs"; Armen A. Alchian and William R. Allen, *Exchange and Production: Competition, Coordination, and Control*, 3rd. ed. (Belmont, Calif.: Wadsworth Publishing, 1983), pp. 4–5. The reduction in future cash flows from higher annual expenditures required in the new state is as real a cost as the proxy solicitation expenditures that Black downplays. By reincorporating, the firm forgoes other opportunities on which those funds could have been spent. Rational decision makers, such as business firms considering reincorporation, include opportunity costs in their cost-benefit calculus. This is finance textbook learning. For example, Brealey and Myers, *Principles of Corporate Finance*, pp. 97–98; Stephen A. Ross, Randolph W. Westerfield, and Jeffrey F. Jaffe, *Corporate Finance*, 3rd ed. (Boston: Irwin, 1993), pp. 186–87.

There is a further difficulty with Black's thesis. It is internally inconsistent. He claims that there is no market for corporate law, because reincorporation costs are trivial, and hence states cannot exploit firms that locate within their jurisdictions. But if Black's contention were correct, there would be no reason for the statistically significant connection between franchise revenues and the responsivenesss of state corporation codes nor for the market's structure—Delaware's large market share, as well as its displacement of New Jersey as the market leader, discussed subsequently in the text. Black's ad hoc explanation of a market structure that is inconsistent with his thesis is to latch on to one of the several factors, judicial expertise, that I develop in a credible commitment explanation of Delaware's success, discussed hereafter; Black, "Is Corporate Law Trivial?" pp. 589–90. But shortly before offering that explanation, he argues that judges have at best only the most marginal of impacts on corporate law, particularly as they will be reversed if they thwart the legislature's will; ibid., pp. 583–85. That is, of course, the clear implication of his thesis of substantive law triviality and no reincorporation costs. But it is ignored when he seeks an alternative explanation for Delaware's success. Black has to explain why judicial decisions matter at all to firms under these circumstances (there should be little need for litigation, as statutes will provide what firms want, otherwise they move costlessly to another state); he does not do so. In fact, he concludes with an acknowledgment that he has not successfully explained Delaware's success; ibid., pp. 590–91.

There is a nonsimultaneity in performance in the charter market that makes firms particularly vulnerable consumers—since firms move first, states could obtain revenues and then not preserve or update their codes up to the point where a firm becomes indifferent between staying and incurring moving costs.

A corporate charter is a relational contract, an association between parties that lasts over a long period during which numerous exchanges occur. Because it continues over a long time and one side's performance is not simultaneous with the other's, unforeseen contingencies are likely to arise over the period of the contract, making it difficult to specify in advance all the parties' rights and obligations. Such a situation therefore presents greater possibilities for an opportunistic breach than a contract for a single simultaneous exchange. The problems for parties in a relational contract are exacerbated when the state is a party, given its additional role as contract enforcer. The party contemplating entering into a long-term contract with the state must consider the additional difficulty that there may be no legal recourse against a contractual breach by the state.

Christopher Grandy provides a good historical example of this difficulty, corporate charters of railroads in New Jersey during the nineteenth century.[12] In the 1830s, New Jersey granted tax concessions to railroads as part of their corporate charters, to spur in-state improvements. As Grandy notes, in contrast to other states, New Jersey neither constructed railroads itself nor invested in private railroad companies but instead played a passive role in economic development, granting contracts in the form of special incorporation acts to private companies that built the state's infrastructure themselves.[13] Because many assets of railroads—tracks, sidings, stations, and so forth—are not redeployable once in place in a state, their value is expropriable through subsequent tax hikes, a vulnerability that is obviated by state ownership of railroad property and that helps to explain the presence of tax-related charter provisions. New Jersey reneged thirty years later and enacted legislation raising taxes on railroads.

---

12. Christopher Grandy, "Can Government Be Trusted to Keep Its Part of a Social Contract? New Jersey and the Railroads, 1825–1888," *Journal of Law, Economics, and Organization*, vol. 5 (1989), p. 249.

13. Ibid., p. 251.

New Jersey courts upheld the tax increase for firms with reservation clauses in their charters (clauses reserving to the state the power to amend a charter) but did not for the four firms whose charters lacked such clauses and were hence considered irrepealable. This contract protection, however, proved ephemeral. The state legislature, at the governor's insistence, enacted legislation to permit the state board of assessors to investigate railroads' alleged underreporting of costs, which threatened to subject them to substantial back taxes and property seizure by the state. Supplemental legislation permitted railroads to waive their claims to irrepealable contracts (and hence tax exemption) in exchange for the state's waiver of its option to seize railroad property. Not surprisingly, only one railroad was investigated by the board under the act, a road with an irrepealable charter. The legislature further changed common practice and conditioned a railroad's enjoyment of an extension of the contractual completion time for construction on waiver of any claims to tax exemption arising from the contract as well as agreement to submit to all future state tax laws and to the state's power to impose a reservation clause on the roads. Confronted with such sharp tactics, the four railroads capitulated, abandoning their rights under their irrepealable charters and submitted to tax increases.[14]

Despite the danger as shown in the New Jersey railroad example, private parties enter into long-term contracts with states all the time. While, in contrast to railroads, firms do not risk physical assets when choosing a statutory domicile, as earlier noted the choice to reincorporate can impose nontrivial costs. For the corporate charter market to work then, the state must be able to offer a credible commitment against opportunistic breach of the relational chartering contract that it will maintain a responsive corporate law regime. Without such a guarantee, the state cannot assure itself of a steady flow of incorporation revenues from migrating firms, let alone charge a premium for a responsive code.

Why Is Delaware Preeminent?

Delaware's preeminence in the corporate charter market results from its ability to resolve credibly the commitment problem in relational

---

14. Ibid., pp. 265–66.

contracting. This ability depends on investing in assets, referred to as transaction-specific assets, whose value is highest when used in a specific relation rather than in any other use.[15] Assets such as these cannot be profitably redeployed, should the original relation be discontinued. In the chartering context, the state must not be able to obtain a return on its investment in the particular asset unless it is successful in procuring incorporations, for the transaction-specific assets have no value besides their use in servicing the needs of domestic firms. This condition protects firms from the state's collecting franchise fees and then behaving opportunistically and repealing desirable provisions in its code, or not amending its code, as changing circumstances require.

The most important transaction-specific asset in the chartering relation is an intangible asset, Delaware's reputation for responsiveness to corporate concerns. It is derived from the substantial revenues that Delaware obtains from corporate franchise taxes: a state with a large proportion of its budget financed by the franchise tax will be responsive to firms, since it has so much to lose. This is because it is extremely difficult, if not impossible, for such a state to maintain its level of services by an alternative revenue source, should it lose incorporations to another state. Delaware's high ratio of franchise taxes to total revenues is, then, an intangible asset that precommits it not to renege on contracts with its corporate customers, for it renders the state equally vulnerable to breach. Delaware is thereby a hostage to its success in the chartering market.

A recent decision by the U.S. Supreme Court provides Delaware with the opportunity to solidify even further its lead in the corporate charter market. In *Delaware v. New York*, the court held that unclaimed dividends and interest, which are assets held in bank and brokerage accounts whose owners cannot be located, are the property of the state of incorporation of the holder of the asset.[16] While only a

---

15. See Oliver E. Williamson, "Credible Commitments: Using Hostages to Support Exchange," *American Economic Review*, vol. 73 (1983), p. 519.

16. 1993 U.S. LEXIS 2553, 61 U.S.L.W. 4295 (March 30, 1993). As the Court noted, however, Congress could alter this allocation rule. It is altogether possible that disappointed states will lobby for a rule less favorable to Delaware, such as the Special Master's choice of the state in which the underlying issuer is headquartered. This occurred with a prior Supreme Court decision in the interstate escheat area, when Congress passed a law concerning the disposition of abandoned money orders

small percentage (0.02) of corporate distributions fall in the category of unclaimed assets, the absolute dollar amounts are substantial: New York escheated $360 million in such funds from 1985 to 1989.[17] One estimate of New York's share of those funds under the Court's statutory domicile rule is $54 million.[18] Because many major securities firms are incorporated in Delaware, much of the remaining amount will go to it. The attorney for Delaware, for example, asserted that New York had informed Delaware that $139 million of the funds escheated through 1988 came from brokers incorporated in Delaware.[19] This is approximately 24 percent of the franchise fees Delaware received over those years, 1985–1988 (see table 1–1).

This hostagelike dependence on franchise tax revenues is not the only mechanism by which Delaware can assure firms that it will not revamp its corporation code to their detriment. Delaware has invested in real assets that have no use outside the chartering business. These assets consist of a comprehensive body of case law, judicial expertise in corporation law, and administrative expertise in the rapid processing of corporate filings.[20] In Delaware, corporate

---

and traveler's checks to override the statutory domicile rule articulated in Pennsylvania v. New York, 407 U.S. 206 (1972). See 88 Stat. 1525, 12 U.S.C. sections 2501–2503.

17. Delaware v. New York, 1993 U.S. LEXIS 2553, 61 U.S.L.W. 4295 (March 30, 1993).

18. Paul M. Barrett, "Justices Deal New York Costly Defeat in Suit by Delaware on Unclaimed Assets," *Wall Street Journal*, March 31, 1993, p. A5.

19. Linda Greenhouse, "Court Ruling over Dividends Pains Albany," *New York Times*, March 31, 1993, p. B1. To the extent New York or another state can establish the last-known addresses of the creditors of the unclaimed assets are in their boundaries, then Delaware will not be able to claim those funds. Delaware v. New York, 1993 U.S. LEXIS 2533, 61 U.S.L.W. 4295 (1993).

20. In prior work, I refer to the importance of the Delaware courts in my credible commitment explanation of Delaware's success in the chartering market, for example, Romano, "Law as a Product," pp. 276–77 ("continuity in and small size of Delaware's chancery court . . . facilitat[es] development of judicial expertise"); ibid., p. 280 ("experienced judges"); Roberta Romano, "The State Competition Debate in Corporate Law," *Cardozo Law Review*, vol. 8 (1987), pp. 709, 722 ("judicial expertise in corporate law"). Bernard Black contends, however, that he offers a new and different explanation of Delaware's success, the expertise of Delaware judges; Black, "Is Corporate Law Trivial," p. 589. Apart from the detail used to develop the thesis, the difference in explanation escapes me.

law cases are heard in the chancery court rather than in courts of general jurisdiction as in other states. The court's small size and continuity in membership facilitate the development of judicial expertise in business law and enhance the predictability of corporate law decisions. Judges are appointed to twelve-year terms by the governor, from a list submitted by a judicial advisory council, with the consent of the senate, and they often have a background in business law.[21] In contrast to life-tenure judges, this appointment process helps to ensure that members of the chancery court will be sensitive to the state's policy of responsiveness in corporate law, since judges who ignore the political consensus in the state will not be reappointed. In addition, having appointed rather than elected judges further facilitates the input in personnel choices of organized groups, such as the corporate bar, which, as discussed, want judges with expertise in business law, as they are more likely to reach decisions that enhance share value.

Delaware's legal capital is a valuable asset to firms, stressed in a survey of corporations reincorporating in Delaware as helpful for planning complex business transactions.[22] Because Delaware could not realize the value of its investment in legal capital in any other use than its incorporation business, as with the dependence on franchise tax revenues this investment increases Delaware's credibility of behaving with sustained responsiveness to firms and also creates an asset independently valued by reincorporating firms. Further, legal capital is not as easily duplicated by other states as the provisions of a corporation code because of the start-up costs in developing expertise and the dynamic precedent-based nature of adjudication by courts. Even if another state were to establish a special court to hear corporate law cases and were to legislate precedential value for Delaware court decisions, it would take considerable time to develop the requisite in-state judicial expertise.[23]

---

21. The connection between the corporate bar and the judiciary was, in fact, one of Cary's principal bases for attacking Delaware. Cary, "Federalism and Corporate Law," pp. 690–92.

22. Romano, "Law as a Product," pp. 258–61, 274–75.

23. Because a rival would necessarily be a small state, so that franchise revenue would have a significant impact on the state budget, the local bar could not provide a pool of experts, while the political process of judicial appointment would surely prevent the employment of prominent out-of-state practitioners as judges.

One might wonder whether Delaware's legal capital is as valuable an asset as I maintain: shareholders are not required to bring lawsuits against Delaware corporations in Delaware, as other state courts can apply Delaware's law. In other words, venue, and not choice-of-law, could be the more determinative factor in litigation outcomes. It turns out, however, that most Delaware firms are in fact sued in Delaware. In the sample of 139 shareholder suits mentioned earlier, of the 68 suits not brought exclusively in federal court, 35 involved Delaware corporations. Twenty-nine of the suits against Delaware firms were filed in the Delaware chancery court (24 exclusively) while 26 of the 33 suits against non-Delaware firms were filed in courts in those firms' incorporation state (14 exclusively).[24] These data make plain that plaintiffs do not perceive it to be undesirable to litigate in Delaware and instead take advantage of its valuable asset of legal capital. They also provide mixed support for Macey and Miller's conjecture concerning a source of Delaware's success, that Delaware's code favors lawyers over shareholders. If their contention is correct, then there should be significantly more filings by domestic corporations in Delaware than in other states. The difference in filings across the two groups of firms is not significant, although there are significantly more exclusive filings in Delaware than in other incorporation states.

The final institutional device by which Delaware maintains its advantage in the corporate charter market is a constitutional provision that requires a supermajority vote of two-thirds of both houses of the legislature to revise its corporation code.[25] This provision makes it difficult for Delaware to renege on the direction of its code. While the provision may well slow the enactment of corporate law reforms, it increases the likelihood that the legal regime can be no worse than

---

24. The thirteen lawsuits not filed in an incorporation state court were filed in courts in the state of the firms' principal place of business or executive office, which typically was also the plaintiff-shareholder's state of residence; in one of these suits, the plaintiff incorrectly alleged that the firm was incorporated in the filing state, New York, when it was actually incorporated in Delaware.

25. Article IX, § 1, which appeared in the Constitution of 1897. The provision had its basis in the voting requirements of the previous state constitution, which predated the general incorporation statute: Article II, § 17 of the Constitution of 1831 required a two-thirds vote of both houses to approve acts of incorporation, except for renewals of existing corporations.

it was at the time of incorporation. This is a desirable feature, if corporations are risk-averse and adopt a strategy toward the choice of statutory domicile that minimizes the worst-case loss. At the same time, the supermajority requirement preserves the personal investments that Delaware's citizens have made in developing skills to service Delaware corporations. It buffers the corporation code by making it difficult for other interests in the state to reverse the direction of public policy radically: only a critical election revolutionizing state politics could do so. Delaware's dependence on franchise tax revenues and the supermajority vote requirement are complementary devices that warrant a responsive corporation code: the former is forward-looking, as the state is goaded to respond to maintain revenues, and the latter is backward-looking, as reversal of policy is made quite difficult. These institutional devices sustain the credibility of Delaware's reputation as a state committed to innovation and responsiveness in corporate law.

History underscores the value of the supermajority provision. At the turn of the century, New Jersey and not Delaware dominated the corporate charter market.[26] As a lame-duck governor about to assume the presidency, Woodrow Wilson had legislation implemented that revamped the state's corporation code; among other reforms, it redefined business trusts, which had been a distinctive New Jersey organizational innovation, and restricted corporate acquisitions and stock ownership.[27] While New Jersey had no comparable supermajority requirement, the parts of the legislation restricting stock ownership and redefining the business trust were enacted by a bare two-thirds margin in the twenty-one member New Jersey senate (14 to 7), and the provision on mergers would not have met Delaware's voting requirement (13 to 6). More important, Wilson's political reforms

---

26. See, for example, Christopher Grandy, "New Jersey Corporate Chartermongering, 1875–1929," *Journal of Economic History*, vol. 49 (1989), p. 677. The corporate charter market had generated sufficient income for New Jersey, at the turn of the century, for it to abolish its property tax. In 1904, after the abolition of the property tax, franchise revenues surpassed 60 percent of the state's receipts. Grandy indicates that the impetus to develop corporate charters as a state product was a fiscal crisis in the late 1880s that had greatly increased state taxes and a political backlash, necessitating the need to locate new revenue sources.

27. Ibid., p. 689.

coincided with changes in the state's economy that reduced the importance of incorporation revenues in its budget.[28]

Delaware, waiting in the wings with a code identical to the former New Jersey statute, stepped in to fill the gap. Four years after its code reform, in 1917, New Jersey repealed and substantially reversed Wilson's legislation, but this action, unsurprisingly, was insufficient to recapture its market position.[29] The state's reneging on its chartering contract made it difficult to convince firms that it would not do so again, and New Jersey no longer was as reliant on corporate franchise taxes to finance its budget. The political impetus for New Jersey's corporation code changes appears to have had an ideological component: electoral successes of the Progressive movement resulted in the enactment of restrictive corporate laws in other states as well, although Delaware did not follow that path.[30]

Some analogous factors involving human capital also tie firms to Delaware, creating a reciprocal hostagelike asset on the corporations' side. Delaware's legal capital provides benefits to corporate lawyers, for it reduces the cost of specialization. Lawyers, and outside counsel in particular, find that their cost of doing business is reduced and

---

28. Ibid. The ratio of total incorporations to in-state manufacturing firms declined, indicating a change in domestic business activity, which Grandy maintains made New Jersey's favorable antitrust corporate law provisions less desirable as they now had a greater instate impact, and as the state's population dramatically increased, the state undertook large-scale infrastructure expenditures, which could not be funded by the revenue stream produced by franchise fees, decreasing the importance of the chartering business as the mainstay of the state's budget.

29. Ibid; see also Ralph Nader, Mark Green, and Joel Seligman, *Taming the Giant Corporation* (New York: Norton, 1976), p. 49.

30. See Elizabeth A. Nunn, "The Evolution of State Corporation Law during the Progressive Era: Case Studies of Delaware, Missouri and Washington" (unpublished manuscript, University of Puget Sound, November 1992). Nunn finds a significant correlation between voting for restrictive corporate laws and a legislator's support for the Progressive party's reform platform in Missouri and Washington. Interestingly, Nunn indicates that the Progressive movement had little influence on Delaware politics. It is difficult to determine whether this finding is a cause or effect of Delaware's leadership in corporate chartering: Delaware's continued responsive corporation code may be a function of the failure of Progressivism in Delaware, or the failure of Progressivism may be due to the economic and institutional factors that made Delaware successful in charter competition.

the value of their human capital depreciates less rapidly when their expertise can be centered on one jurisdiction, in particular a jurisdiction in which legal outcomes are more predictable. Thus, they have incentives to advise clients to move to Delaware, and once there not to relocate, because moving diminishes their legal capital. Indeed, in a survey of firms' reincorporation decisions, outside counsel was more frequently involved in a decision to move when the destination state was Delaware, as opposed to another state.[31] If a firm relocates, its attorney cannot recoup investments in mastering Delaware law, and the cost of providing advice rises with retooling. Delaware also aids the bar in maintaining its human capital by circulating unpublished court opinions and by consulting prominent members of the bar, outside as well as inside the state, on corporate law revisions. These advantages for lawyers benefit shareholders by reducing the cost of legal services.

Delaware and firms are thereby joined in a long-term relationship because of reciprocal vulnerability—the loss of investments in human and legal capital—that cements Delaware's market position while making it difficult for another state to compete. Offering Delaware's code at a lower price will not enable another state to attract incorporations: a switch increases a firm's legal costs, and a rival state cannot credibly precommit to superior service, as Delaware has done by its investments and budgetary position. A rival begins from a lower franchise tax ratio and incurs start-up costs of developing legal capital. Thus, Delaware has a first-mover advantage in the corporate charter business.

Once Delaware established its dominant position, it became cheaper for it to maintain a commanding lead over a newcomer, because there is value in numbers. The more firms there are in Delaware, the more franchise tax receipts it receives and the more it will rely on its charter business, making it even more important to be responsive. In addition, the more firms there are in Delaware, the more legal precedents will be produced, further providing a sounder basis for business planning, which attracts even more firms to that state. Finally, the more corporate law cases that are brought, the greater will be the expertise of the Delaware judges, as will be the value to an individual from developing such expertise as a member of the judiciary.

---

31. Romano, "Law as a Product," pp. 274–75.

Alternative Explanations of the Chartering Market

An alternative explanation of Delaware's success in the corporate chartering market to the transaction-oriented explanation offered here views corporation codes as heterogeneous products through which states appeal to dissimilar types of firms by offering diverse products: different default rules for corporate charters. Richard Posner and Kenneth Scott, in a note in their corporate law reader, for example, have suggested that Delaware specializes in charters for large public corporations, given the higher cost of a Delaware incorporation for small firms.[32]

Competing state codes are not, however, necessary to sort firms by size, because a single state can offer separate codes for differently sized firms. As noted, Delaware, like many states, has special code provisions for close corporations. In addition, only about half of the largest firms are incorporated in Delaware. Size alone is therefore not a distinguishing characteristic for a Delaware domicile. Comparison of a number of attributes of large firms incorporated in Delaware and in other states shows no statistically significant differences except the number of acquisitions made by the firms (which is higher for Delaware-domiciled firms.)[33] This finding is more consistent with this monograph's explanation of moves to Delaware when firms expect to engage in transactions whose costs are reduced by being subject to Delaware's code than with a straightforward size explanation.

Barry Baysinger and Henry Butler offer another product differentiation story. They contend that variations in corporation codes match divergent capital structures, and in particular, that corporations with more concentrated share ownership will prefer strict codes providing less discretion to managers than Delaware's code.[34] To

---

32. Richard A. Posner and Kenneth E. Scott, *Economics of Corporation Law and Securities Regulation* (Boston: Little Brown, 1980), p. 111.

33. Romano, "Law as a Product," pp. 261–65.

34. Barry D. Baysinger and Henry N. Butler, "The Role of Corporate Law in the Theory of the Firm," *Journal of Law and Economics*, vol. 28 (1985), p. 179. Easterbrook and Fischel reinterpret Baysinger and Butler's thesis into a more plausible contention that smaller firms will prefer strict codes over Delaware's code, because their investors cannot rely on capital markets to monitor management; Easterbrook and Fischel, *Economic Structure of Corporate Law*, p. 216. Easterbrook

reach such a conclusion, Baysinger and Butler assume that holders of blocks of stock will not run the firm and that such investors find it difficult to sell if dissatisfied with management, because the sale of a block is expected to depress the market, at least temporarily. Consequently, blockholders must rely on the internal governance mechanism of a strict code rather than the market for protection from management expropriation.

To test their hypothesis, Baysinger and Butler defined a strict corporation code as a code in a state from which New York and American Stock Exchange–listed corporations migrate to Delaware, rather than by analysis of code provisions. They then compared ownership characteristics of firms incorporated in the states they identified as strict with those of firms that have migrated from those states. The categorization of states as strict from migration patterns is, however, problematic. In particular, it is inconsistent with the index of code responsiveness to corporate demands, discussed earlier, that I constructed based on the substantive content of state corporation codes.[35] Hence, although they find, as they predicted, that the firms that did not move have a higher percentage of block ownership (but not a higher percentage of shares owned by officers and directors) than those that did change domicile, it is not obvious whether this difference is related to a corporation code's relative substantive strictness.[36]

---

and Fischel's interpretation is an accurate representation of Baysinger and Butler's thesis to the extent that large firms have more diffuse equity ownership than small firms, for then Baysinger and Butler's concentrated ownership variable is a proxy for firm size. In this view of the thesis, we expect block holders to be better able to monitor managers than dispersed shareholders (monitoring costs are spread across more shares), and presumably strict codes enable such investors to monitor managers more effectively.

35. The differences are discussed in detail in Romano, "The State Competition Debate," p. 715.

36. Baysinger and Butler also find that financial performance does not differ across the two groups of firms in their sample, which is consistent with a sorting explanation—firms choose the code that maximizes value given their capital structure—rather than either Cary's or Winter's position on state competition, which would predict, respectively, worse or better performance by migrating firms. The significance and persuasiveness of the conclusion are, however, as equally undercut by the inadequacy of the code classification system as is the finding of ownership differences, for the failure to find a difference in performance may be

There is another, more plausible explanation for a connection between concentrated ownership and frequency of reincorporation that is independent of Baysinger and Butler's characterization of state codes and relates their sorting hypothesis to the transaction hypothesis: when ownership of a firm is concentrated, the explicit provisions of a corporation code do not matter much, because a controlling shareholder, and hence management, can implement chosen policies without difficulty regardless of the statutory provisions (they have control of the firm). There is thus no reason to move to incur the higher costs of a Delaware domicile until the owners anticipate undertaking new activities, or reducing control, whereupon legal rules will loom larger. From this perspective, Baysinger and Butler's product differentiation or sorting explanation and this monograph's transaction explanation of the structure of the chartering market are complementary, not competing explanations.

There is, however, a fundamental weakness in the product differentiation story in contrast to this monograph's explanation. A product differentiation explanation of the chartering market is premised on significant diversity in state corporation codes to match different types of business firms. But there is a high degree of uniformity in state codes. In particular, innovations in corporate laws diffuse gradually across the states, including innovations by Delaware.[37] Such a pattern of convergence would not be prominent if firms' tastes so varied that states could profitably distinguish themselves by corporation codes. Both the classic positions in the debate over state competiton for corporate charters are consistent with the extant uniformity of codes: a race for the top or for the bottom results in copycat statutes, as the worst or best (depending on the perspective) statutes are winnowed out over time by experimentation. This monograph's transaction-based explanation is also consonant with uniform codes. Competing states respond to the tastes of transaction-oriented firms concerned about litigation; they can cheaply replicate Delaware's code (hence we see substantial uniformity in state codes),

---

due to classification errors (improperly differentiating states whose codes are similar).

37. Romano, "Law as a Product," pp. 233–35 (diffusion of several corporate law reforms); Romano "Corporate Governance," p. 1160 (diffusion of Delaware limited liability statute).

but they cannot as easily duplicate its court system with its evolving body of precedents or franchise fee advantage (hence Delaware retains its market share).

The Dynamism of Federalism

Why did I refer at the outset to federalism as the genius of American corporate law? None of the important transaction-specific assets on the state side that solidify Delaware's commanding position and safeguard the concerns of firms would be present in a system of national corporate chartering. Given the sheer size of the federal budget, there would be no revenue incentive to constrain the national government from behaving opportunistically by, for instance, installing high franchise fees without delivering laws that corporations prefer. And in the absence of a corporate law court, there would be no parallel protection of nonredeployable legal capital, for there would be no opportunity to develop the requisite judicial expertise. More important, there would be no competition prodding the national government to improve its service (unless the cost of using the partnership form or incorporation in a foreign country is considerably reduced from present levels) and cheaply informing it about the value of alternative approaches to corporate organization. Accordingly, the dynamism of federalism—the superior ability to adjust to changing circumstances—would be lost.

The establishment of a specialized national court of corporate law would not eliminate the disadvantage of a national regime, for it is more difficult to reverse judicial mistakes in this setting. Congress has many more policy concerns and takes far longer to act than a state legislature. Even with a will to be responsive, implementing national legislation is more difficult than taking state action. The support of more legislators must be obtained, as just the number of members of the U.S. House of Representatives (435) alone is greater than the number of legislators in both houses in the state with the largest number of legislators (424 in New Hampshire; the next largest legislature, Pennsylvania's, totals only 253 legislators).[38] Congres-

---

38. Council of State Governments, *The Book of the States*, 1990–1991 ed. (Lexington, Ky.: CSG, 1990), p. 123.

sional specialization through the use of committees mitigates the coordination problem, but it does not improve the congressional legislative process relative to that of the states, especially a state whose attention is focused by franchise tax revenues. A study of congressional reversals of Supreme Court decisions invalidating federal statutes, for example, found a lapse of 2.4 years from judicial opinion to reversal.[39] The Delaware legislature has acted far more quickly to reverse undesirable decisions: the limited liability statute discussed earlier was enacted 1.5 years after a controversial decision, *Smith v. Van Gorkom*,[40] which held that directors breached their duty of care in accepting an acquisition offer at a substantial premium.

Van Gorkom—one of the few cases to find directors liable for negligence—created substantial uncertainty concerning how Delaware's fiduciary standard was to be applied.[41] In addition, the case was decided at a time when the market for directors' and officers' liability insurance (which covers directors' and officers' expenses in certain third-party and shareholder suits) was in turmoil, with premiums skyrocketing as coverage was contracting.[42] There was, not surprisingly, a strong critical reaction to the opinion, as firms feared able individuals would refuse to serve on boards. The Delaware legislature resolved the problem created by the opinion: it permitted firms to opt out of the decision by eliminating or limiting directors' liability for negligence.

The absence of a budgetary incentive or competitors that can offer an alternative to spark either innovation or imitation could be offset if members of Congress would be disciplined (that is, experienced a diminished likelihood of reelection) if they were not responsive to firms, and, in particular, to policies that enhance share value. Quite apart from the power of incumbency, through which more than 90 percent of members of Congress seeking reelection retain their

---

39. See Thomas R. Marshall, *Public Opinion and the Supreme Court* (Boston: Unwin Hyman, 1989), p. 169.

40. 488 A.2d 858 (Del. 1985).

41. Roberta Romano, "What Went Wrong with Directors' and Officers' Liability Insurance?" *Delaware Journal of Corporate Law*, vol. 14 (1989), pp. 1, 23–24.

42. Ibid.

seats,[43] corporate law problems are not salient issues for the voting public. It is therefore problematic whether members of an inattentive Congress, with far greater coordination difficulties than state legislatures, would suffer adverse electoral consequences from maintaining a low level of responsiveness in corporate law. The more realistic scenario, given the indifference of the voting public, is that the same forces affecting state legislation will affect Congress. Hence, even if a modified version of Cary's analysis were accurate and state legislatures catered to managers to the detriment of shareholders, the political dynamics in the national arena indicate that Congress would cater to managers as well. Shareholders dispersed across fifty states and the District of Columbia have no greater incentive to lobby in Congress than in Delaware, where many firms are located.

The most compelling case for national regulation of corporate law involves state takeover statutes, which govern transactions where managers' and shareholders' interests can diverge sharply. This is the one area of legislation where empirical studies support Cary's characterization of state codes: researchers have found significant negative stock price effects on enactment of certain takeover statutes in a number of states, although not in Delaware.[44] If national regulation cannot be justified even in this apparently compelling context, then comprehensive reform proposals finding fault with state competition and advocating across-the-board national corporation laws ought to be approached with considerable skepticism.[45] Chapter

---

43. James Q. Wilson, *American Government*, 4th ed. (Lexington, Mass.: D. C. Heath & Co., 1989), p. 276. The reelection rate of senators is substantially lower (75 percent); ibid., p. 277. There is a similar incumbency advantage in state legislatures. A study of elections in sixteen states with single-member legislative districts shows that 93 percent of House and 89 percent of Senate incumbents are reelected; James C. Garand, "Electoral Marginality in State Legislative Elections, 1968–86," *Legal Studies Quarterly*, vol. 16 (1991), pp. 7, 12. In Delaware, the winning proportions for House and Senate are, respectively, 91 percent and 93 percent; ibid. The reelection rate does not indicate that incumbents with safe seats can disregard their constituents' preferences and vote as they wish. Rather it suggests that they are reelected with such large margins precisely because they are responsive to their constituents. The key factors for determining how incumbents will react to corporate law policies are therefore the two other factors discussed in the text, the saliency of the issue and the organization of interest groups.

44. The studies are summarized in table 4–1 in chapter 4.

45. For example, Bebchuk, "Federalism and the Corporation." Bebchuk maintains that some areas are appropriate for state competition and others are not, but his

4 evaluates whether the favorable assessment of state competition for charters that has been outlined thus far is shaken by state takeover regulation.

---

exceptions appear to swallow the rule, because he places virtually all of corporate law (takeover regulation, fiduciary duties, proxy contests, dividend policy, board representation) under national jurisdiction.

4

Takeover Statutes as Anomalies or Paradigms of Corporate Law?

TAKEOVER REGULATION involves the subset of state laws most troubling to proponents of state competition, for in contrast to most corporation code contexts, the conflict of interest between managers and shareholders in the takeover setting is stark. In a takeover, management is placed in an endgame situation in which benefiting shareholders by supporting a bid that provides a hefty premium need not increase the manager's welfare because of the increased prospect of loss of employment on a bid's success. While target shareholders experience abnormal returns ranging between 20 and 40 percent in takeovers,[1] managers are frequently replaced; studies find a higher than average turnover in management after a takeover, particularly after a contested takeover.[2] Indeed, the larger the change in management's wealth from a takeover (that is, the larger its stock and option holdings), indicating that its interests in a bid are more closely

---

1. For reviews of studies on returns to target shareholders, see Michael C. Jensen and Richard S. Ruback, "The Market for Corporate Control: The Scientific Evidence," *Journal of Financial Economics*, vol. 11 (1980), p. 5; Gregg A. Jarrell, James A. Brickley, and Jeffry M. Netter, "The Market for Corporate Control: The Empirical Evidence since 1980," *Journal of Economic Perspectives*, vol. 2 (Winter 1988), p. 49. The best available evidence is that takeover gains are efficiency-related and not wealth transfers from other participants in the firm; see Roberta Romano, "A Guide to Takeovers: Theory, Evidence and Regulation," *Yale Journal on Regulation*, vol. 9 (1992), p. 119.

2. For a review of studies on management turnover, see Eugene Furtado and Vijay Karan, "Causes, Consequences, and the Shareholder Wealth Effects of Management Turnover: A Review of Empirical Evidence," *Financial Management*, vol. 19 (1990), p. 60.

aligned with those of shareholders, the less likely it is to resist a takeover.[3]

In addition to the agency problem, jurisdictional spillovers in the form of negative externalities—effects on third parties outside the manager-shareholder relation, such as employees and local communities—are thought to be present in the takeover context. As has been discussed, this is a conventional argument against federalism and for national regulation. The benefits of state competition would therefore appear problematic in the context of laws regulating takeovers.

A Review of Takeover Regulation

Takeover regulation in the United States is an area of dual jurisdiction. The ground rules for tender offers are set forth in national legislation, the Williams Act, which was enacted in 1968.[4] Its main components are (1) substantive regulation of terms and procedures for bids, such as requirements of withdrawal rights, pro rata acceptance of shares if a bid is oversubscribed, and regulation of extensions and changes in bids; (2) prebid disclosure, on acquisition of 5 percent of the common stock in a corporation, of the shares' ownership and financing and the purpose of the acquisition; and (3) antifraud provisions covering communications concerning an offer by bidders and incumbent management. The primary benefit of the act from management's perspective is that it facilitates delay by, for example, providing opportunities for litigation alleging material misstatements or omissions in disclosure documents. If target management is successful in a preliminary hearing, it obtains an injunction, halting a bid's progress temporarily, until a trial on the merits or until a flawed disclosure is corrected. This is often akin to defeating a bid, because delay permits competing bidders to come forward (management has time to locate a white knight, a more preferred partner) or enables management to restructure defensively to avoid acquisition.

---

3. Ralph A. Walkling and Michael S. Long, "Agency Theory, Managerial Welfare, and Takeover Bid Resistance," *RAND Journal of Economics*, vol. 15 (1984), p. 54.

4. Act of July 29, 1968, Pub.L. No. 90-439, 82 Stat. 454, amending the Securities Exchange Act of 1934, 15 U.S.C. §§ 78a et seq. The act was further amended in 1970.

Shareholders can benefit from delay if competition increases the bid price. This benefit may be more apparent than real, however, for increasing the initial bidders' costs will reduce the number of bids (there are fewer bids, because the likelihood of a bidder recovering the cost of searching for a target is lowered as another bidder can free ride on the first and, not having similar search costs to recoup, outbid it), which lowers shareholder welfare.[5] Moreover, in more than 20 percent of takeover contests in which management employed litigation as a defensive maneuver, the target remained independent on defeating the bid, and shareholders received no premium.[6]

At approximately the same time as the enactment of the Williams Act, Virginia adopted the first state takeover statute. Thereafter, many states intervened in takeovers, with the pace of legislation accelerating in the mid-1970s, as the number of takeovers increased.[7] Finding the Williams Act inadequate as a defense against takeovers, states sought to fashion rules that were even more favorable to incumbent managements. Under the first generation of state laws, tender offerors had to submit plans to a state agency and obtain approval before proceeding with bids. This regulation was far more advantageous to management than a preliminary injunction against a bidder for violation of the Williams Act, because state review tended to be extremely protracted.

Bidders quickly attacked state takeover statutes, using two arguments related to the supremacy of the national government over the states: (1) they amounted to an unconstitutional state burden on interstate commerce and (2) they were preempted by the Williams Act. The issue was preliminarily resolved in 1982, in *Edgar v. MITE*,[8] when the Supreme Court found that first-generation takeover

---

5. Frank H. Easterbrook and Daniel R. Fischel, "The Proper Role of a Target's Management in Responding to a Tender Offer," *Harvard Law Review*, vol. 94 (1981), p. 1161; Alan Schwartz, "Search Theory and the Tender Offer Auction," *Journal of Law, Economics, and Organization*, vol. 2 (1986), p. 229. The effect of takeover auctions on shareholder welfare has been roundly debated. For a review of the debate, see Romano, "Guide to Takeovers."

6. Gregg Jarrell, "The Wealth Effects of Litigation by Targets: Do Interests Diverge in a Merge?" *Journal of Law and Economics*, vol. 28 (1985), p. 151.

7. See Roberta Romano, "The Future of Hostile Takeovers: Legislation and Public Opinion," *University of Cincinnati Law Review*, vol. 57 (1988), pp. 457, 458–60.

8. 457 U.S. 624 (1982).

regulation burdened interstate commerce; a plurality of justices considered such statutes preempted as well.

States were not, however, deterred by *MITE* from intervening in bids. They quickly fashioned new regulations, known as second-generation statutes. The new statutes exhibited greater diversity in approach than first-generation statutes. The most prominent of such laws restrict the voting rights of bidders' shares without the other shareholders' approval (control share acquisition statutes), limit bidders' ability to engage in business combinations and other related transactions with targets after a bid's success (business combination freeze statutes), and require bidders to pay at least as much for shares in the second stage of a two-tier acquisition as they paid in the first stage (fair price statutes).

In contrast to first-generation statutes, second-generation statutes regulate matters that fall into the legal category of a corporation's internal affairs, which are the province of the incorporation state. Such an approach was considered a constitutionally acceptable means of avoiding *MITE's* strictures. Regulating matters of internal affairs, that is, corporate governance, was considered a valid exercise of state power despite a potential impact on commerce, for it did not meet the *MITE* Court's tests of unconstitutionality. First, the jurisdictional basis of first-generation statutes, presence of assets in the state, had an unconstitutional extraterritorial effect,[9] as a firm with operations in several states could be subject to inconsistent regulations, whereas the jurisdiction of the second-generation statutes depends on incorporation state, which avoids such an unconstitutional effect. Second, unlike first-generation statutes, the new laws

---

9. Judge Ralph Winter distinguished first-generation takeover statutes from state competition over corporate codes because of their extraterritorial effect (they applied to firms with plants located in the legislating state, not solely to domestically incorporated corporations). He maintained that this jurisdictional provision enabled states to restrain the competition for charters and thus to enact shareholder-wealth-decreasing laws; Winter, "State Law, Shareholder Protection and the Theory of the Corporation," pp. 268, 287–89. Subsequent-generation takeover statutes do not have such broad jurisdictional hooks and consequently pose analytical problems for state competition advocates. In a recent comment, Winter recognized this point, noting that some states (particularly those regulating takeovers) may not seek to maximize franchise tax revenues, and hence the "race to the top [may be a] walk"; Ralph K. Winter, "The 'Race for the Top' Revisited: A Comment on Eisenberg," *Columbia Law Review*, vol. 89 (1989), pp. 1526, 1528–29.

did not discriminate against out-of-state shareholders: the shares of all bidders, regardless of domicile, were equally affected by the statutes. In fact, the *MITE* Court emphasized that Illinois could have "no interest in regulating the internal affairs of foreign corporations." This reasoning lent powerful support to the new approach. Furthermore, by phrasing their legislation as regulating internal affairs, states ensured that the question of preemption could not be revived. Corporate internal affairs are conventionally considered in the states' exclusive sphere of authority, and the Williams Act was not regarded as having altered the historical regulatory balance between Congress and the states.

After a series of lower court decisions invalidating control share acquisition statutes, in 1987 the Supreme Court upheld Indiana's version in *CTS Corp. v. Dynamics Corp. of America.*[10] This decision made clear that states have a role in takeover regulation. After the decision, takeover statutes proliferated. States continued to innovate, enacting multiple takeover statutes that provided firms with an extensive menu of defensive protections. The most recent form, adopted in more than half of the states, permits or requires corporate boards to consider the interests of nonshareholder groups in their decisions (other-constituency statutes). The most Draconian new statute is Pennsylvania's 1990 disgorgement statute, which prohibits failed bidders from earning a profit on the sale of their shares. By the early 1990s, with the acquisitions market at a standstill, the pace of legislative activity slowed as well.

Second-generation statutes often codify defensive tactics that firms can undertake voluntarily by charter amendment. A disturbing feature of such statutes is that they allow managers to engage in such defensive tactics without first seeking a charter amendment and, correspondingly, shareholder approval. Almost all second-generation statutes permit firms to opt out of coverage rather than require them to opt in affirmatively. The difference between opting out and opting in is important, because management has an advantage in using the proxy machinery over shareholders. Management's proxy expenses are paid for by firms as incurred, whereas challengers' expenses are reimbursed only if they are successful in gaining control and thus are in a position to propose reimbursing themselves. Management is

---

10. 481 U.S. 69 (1987).

unlikely to propose that the corporation defray the expenses of its opposition. Because an investor's pro rata benefit will not cover solicitation costs, the investor is less likely to propose an amendment (in states where management's initiation is not required) than management. The shareholders' collective choice problem is thus exacerbated in the opt-out setting, where shareholder initiative is required. This managerial advantage is of particular concern in the takeover context, because it affects the outcome of bidding contests (statutory coverage is intended to increase bidding costs and hence to reduce the probability of a bid's success).

The Politics of Takeover Statutes

The politics of takeover statutes is consistent with an agency problem. The potential losers in takeovers—top management—are the principal promoters of the legislation. Takeover laws are typically sponsored by the state chamber of commerce at the behest of a major local corporation that is the target of a hostile bid.[11] Such laws are often rapidly enacted, sometimes over a few days in special emergency sessions, depending on the urgency of the situation of the firm seeking the legislation. Moveover, the statutes are usually enacted without public hearings. Legislators' support is bipartisan and nearly unanimous.

Takeover statutes are not, as some might suspect, promoted by a broad coalition of business, labor, and community leaders who fear that a change in control will have a detrimental effect on the local economy. While union representatives endorse takeover legislation in some states, in the vast majority the only organized group interested in the legislation besides management is the corporate bar. Anecdotal accounts suggest that the roles of these latter two groups are reversed when contrasted to the usual legislative process of corporate law reform: business lobbying organizations lead the way in takeover statutes, whereas the bar is the prime mover behind most changes in corporation codes.

The absence of broad-based lobbying for takeover statutes does

---

11. For a listing of firms and states, see Henry Butler, "Corporation-Specific Anti-Takeover Statutes and the Market for Corporate Charters," *Wisconsin Law Review* (1988), p. 365; Romano, "Future of Hostile Takeovers," p. 461 n. 11.

not mean that legislators voting for statutes are not motivated by a concern for saving local jobs. But if workers' employment, as opposed to management's, is the primary motivation of legislators, the concern is not well founded. In measuring the effect of takeovers on employment and wages, numerous studies have failed to find a detrimental impact on labor: takeovers generally do not affect the employment of production workers nor do they reduce union wages.[12] In the small set of cases where labor suffers losses (primarily reductions in administrative staff employment, thinning the ranks of middle managers), the loss is a small fraction of the bid premium (10–20 percent).[13]

Moreover, a close examination of the political process of takeover legislation raises a serious question whether employee welfare is a concern in the first place. Business groups that are the moving force behind takeover statutes vigorously oppose plant-closing legislation, and takeover statutes regulating severance pay and union contract security are careful to exempt friendly acquisitions. In addition, other-constituency statutes do not provide workers with the right to enforce the statute against a board that does not consider their interest or does not act in their favor. If job security of employees, rather than top management, were the true concern, we would not observe such carefully crafted distinctions.

Like most pork-barrel legislation such as public works ("rivers and harbors") bills, takeover statutes are almost always unanimously approved.[14] The likely explanation for such legislative unanimity is

12. For example, Frank R. Lichtenberg and Donald Siegel, "The Effects of Ownership Changes on the Employment and Wages of Central Office and Other Personnel," *Journal of Law and Economics*, vol. 33 (1990), p. 383; Joshua G. Rosett, "Do Union Wealth Concessions Explain Takeover Premiums? The Evidence on Contract Wages," *Journal of Financial Economics*, vol. 27 (1990), p. 263. For a nontechnical review of the now extensive literature on the impact of takeovers on employees, see Romano, "Guide to Takeovers."

13. For example, Sanjai Bhagat, Andrei Shleifer, and Robert W. Vishny, "Hostile Takeovers in the 1980s: The Return to Corporate Specialization," in M. N. Bailey and C. Whinston, eds., *Brookings Papers on Economic Activity: Microeconomics 1990 #1* (Washington, D.C.: Brookings Institution, 1990), p. 1.

14. Classic studies finding outcomes approaching unanimity for pork barrel project legislation include John A. Ferejohn, *Pork Barrel Politics: Rivers and Harbors Legislation 1947–1968* (Stanford: Stanford University Press, 1974); Douglas R. Arnold, *Congress and the Bureaucracy: A Theory of Influence* (New Haven: Yale

that the benefits and beneficiaries (real or supposed) of such legislation are highly concentrated—many, if not most, of the target company's managers and workers reside within the state—while the costs are borne largely by a loosely organized, geographically dispersed group, shareholders. Viewed in this light, unanimity in the enactment of takeover statutes may represent a disadvantage of federalism, as noted, that the benefits and burdens of a law may not be contained within the legislating jurisdiction. When such spillover effects occur, interjurisdictional subsidization and exploitation can occur, as citizens of the legislating state benefit from a law while citizens of other states bear the cost. This is the theoretical underpinning of the case for national regulation. [15]

Delaware's Unique Position

A striking anomaly in state takeover regulation is that in this context alone Delaware has been slower to respond than other states. It enacted a first-generation statute in 1975, seven years and six states after Virginia's pioneering legislation, and it did not adopt a second-generation statute until after the Supreme Court's *CTS* decision. On most major corporate law reforms, by contrast, it has been either the first or second to act. [16] In addition, both of Delaware's takeover statutes have been less restrictive of hostile bids than those of other states. Its first-generation statute, for instance, did not have a hearing requirement, and, unlike other state laws, it had an opt-out provision. Its second-generation statute bans business combinations for only three years (compared with New York's five years) and can be avoided entirely if an acquirer obtains 85 percent of the stock in the transaction in which it becomes interested.

Several important features related to the issue of interjurisdictional spillovers distinguish Delaware from other states and help explain the differences in its takeover statutes and the timing of their enactment. First, Delaware has a more diverse corporate constitu-

University Press, 1979); and Richard F. Fenno, *Congressmen in Committees* (Boston: Little, Brown, 1973).

15. See Saul Levmore, "Interstate Exploitation and Judicial Intervention," *Virginia Law Review*, vol. 69 (1983), p. 563.

16. See Romano, "Law as a Product."

ency, which includes both target companies and bidders, than other states, which makes the legislative process less one-sided. In fact, there is a significant negative correlation between a state's having been at the forefront in enacting a second-generation statute before *CTS* was decided, which is an indicium of an aggressive antitakeover regulatory stance, and the number of hostile bidders incorporated in the state.[17] Second, the large number of incorporated firms in Delaware, few of which are physically present in the state, means that no one firm's management has the clout to get a bill enacted. This also makes it cheaper for shareholder groups and institutional investors to lobby the Delaware legislature, as the cost is spread over a large number of portfolio holdings.

Third, and finally, although it is not a formal requirement all legislation on corporate law in Delaware is initiated, reviewed, and formally approved by the bar before introduction in the legislature. The diverse interests represented by the Delaware bar at the earliest stages of legislation make it more difficult to enact statutes with unintended consequences and mitigate the harmful effects on shareholders of takeover laws that are enacted. The Delaware bar represents a far broader set of constituent interests than the corporate bar in other states (bidders as well as targets have local Delaware counsel). In other states, the local corporate bar tends to be more aligned with incumbent management, because when firms merge, the acquirer's counsel typically remains the combined entity's counsel.

Effects of Takeover Regulation on Shareholder Wealth

Empirical research on the effects of takeover laws on shareholder wealth is most consistent with Cary's view of the harmful effect of state competition. Event studies find either statistically significant negative stock price effects or no effect (as summarized in table 4–1).[18] The most comprehensive event study of takeover statutes, by

---

17. Roberta Romano, "The Political Economy of Takeover Statutes," *Virginia Law Review*, vol. 73 (1987), pp. 111, 142–45.

18. Studies finding significant negative stock price effects are Adam Broner, *New Jersey Shareholders Protection Act: An Economic Evaluation, A Report to the New Jersey Legislature* (Trenton, N.J.: Office of Economic Policy, State of New Jersey, 1987); Jonathan Karpoff and Paul Malatesta, "The Wealth Effects of Second-Generation State Takeover Legislation," *Journal of Financial Economics*, vol. 25

Jonathan Karpoff and Paul Malatesta, examined the stock price effects of forty second-generation statutes enacted through 1987 (all legislation with press coverage). They find a small statistically significant decrease in stock price (− .3 percent) over the two-day interval of the earliest press reports of proposed legislation.[19]

In the Karpoff and Malatesta study, there is no significant stock price effect on important dates in the statutes' legislative histories (bill introduction, floor votes, gubernatorial signing) that are not simultaneously covered in the press. There is also no significant effect over longer intervals around press report dates. When the

---

(1989), p. 291; Jonathan Karpoff and Paul Malatesta, "PA: State Antitakeover Laws and Stock Prices," *Financial Analysts Journal*, vol. 46 (July–August 1990), p. 8; Charles R. Mahla, Jr., *State Takeover Statutes and Shareholder Wealth* (Ph.D. diss., University of North Carolina, 1991); Donald G. Margotta, "Stock Price Effects of Pennsylvania Act 36" (unpublished manuscript, Northeastern University, 1991); Michael Ryngaert and Jeffry Netter, "Shareholder Wealth Effects of the Ohio Antitakeover Law," *Journal of Law, Economics, and Organization*, vol. 4 (1988), p. 373; Michael Ryngaert and Jeffry Netter, "Shareholder Wealth Effects of the 1986 Ohio Antitakeover Law Revisited: Its Real Effects," *Journal of Law, Economics, and Organization*, vol. 6 (1990), p. 253; Laurence Schumann, "State Regulation of Takeovers and Shareholder Wealth: The Effects of New York's 1985 Takeover Statutes," *RAND Journal of Economics*, vol. 19 (1988), p. 557; Sidak and Woodward, "Corporate Takeovers, the Commerce Clause, and the Efficient Anonymity of Shareholders," p. 1092; Samuel H. Szewczyk and George P. Tsetsekos, "State Intervention in the Market for Corporate Control: The Case of Pennsylvania Senate Bill 1310," *Journal of Financial Economics*, vol. 31 (1992), p. 3.

Studies finding no significant effects are John S. Jahera and William N. Pugh, "State Takeover Legislation: The Case of Delaware," *Journal of Law, Economics, and Organization*, vol. 7 (1991), p. 410; Donald G. Margotta and Swaminathan Badrinath, "Effects of New Jersey Shareholder Protection Legislation on Stock Prices" (unpublished manuscript, Northwestern University, 1987); Donald G. Margotta, Thomas P. McWilliams, and Victoria B. McWilliams, "An Analysis of the Stock Price Effect of the 1986 Ohio Takeover Legislation," *Journal of Law, Economics, and Organization*, vol. 6 (1990), p. 235; William N. Pugh and John S. Jahera, "State Antitakeover Legislation and Shareholder Wealth," *Journal of Financial Research*, vol. 13 (1990), p. 221; Romano, "Political Economy of Takeover Statutes"; Roberta Romano, "What Is the Value of Other Constituency Statutes to Shareholders?" *University of Toronto Law Journal*, vol. 67 (forthcoming). Note that some of the studies in the latter category, such as Margotta and Badrinath, do find significant negative effects for certain event intervals but not for others and therefore conclude that the laws have no detrimental wealth effects.

19. Karpoff and Malatesta, "Wealth Effects of Second-Generation State Takeover Legislation," pp. 308–9.

TABLE 4–1
EVENT STUDIES OF TAKEOVER STATUTES

Type of Statute	State	Effect on Stock Prices
Multiple Statute		
Karpoff and Malatesta (1989)	40 statutes in 26 states	Negative CAR over 2-day press date event interval
Mahla (1991)	49 statutes in 30 states	Negative AR at day 3 and day 2; negative AR at day 0 significant only at .10; for statutes enacted pre-CTS decision, negative AR at day 0
Pugh and Jahera (1990)	5 statutes and 1 vetoed bill in 4 states	No significant effect; negative CAR on introduction date and 2-day interval significant only at .10
Business Combination Freeze Statute		
Karpoff and Malatesta (1989)	Multiple statutes	Negative CAR over 2-day press date event interval
Mahla (1991)	Multiple statutes	Negative AR day 0
Karpoff and Malatesta (1989)	Del.	No significant effect
Jahera and Pugh (1991)	Del.	Positive CAR over 8 separate 2-day event intervals
Pugh and Jahera (1990)	Ind.	No significant effect
Broner (1987)	N.J.	Negative CAR 10 days around Senate committee approval
Margotta and Badrinath (1987)	N.J.	No significant effect
Pugh and Jahera (1990)	N.J.	No significant effect
Schumann (1988)	N.Y.	Negative CAR over 3-day legislative event interval
Karpoff and Malatesta (1989)	N.Y.	No significant effect
Pugh and Jahera (1990)	N.Y.	Positive CAR between introduction and passage by first chamber; otherwise no significant effect

Control Share Acquisition Statute

Study	State(s)	Result
Karpoff and Malatesta (1989)	Multiple statutes	No significant effect
Mahla (1991)	Multiple statutes	No significant effect, positive AR day-4
Karpoff and Malatesta (1989)	Ind.	Negative CAR over 2-day press date event interval
Pugh and Jahera (1990)	Ind.	Negative CAR on introduction date; insignificant CAR at other legislative event dates
Sidak and Woodward (1990)	Ind.	Negative CAR on legislative event dates
Romano (1987)	Mo.	No significant effect
Schumann (1988)	N.Y.[a]	Negative CAR over 88-day interval up to governor's veto date; positive CAR significant only at .06 over 3-day interval around veto
Pugh and Jahera (1990)	N.Y.[a]	Negative CAR on passage by second chamber
Pugh and Jahera (1990)	Ohio	No significant effect
Karpoff and Malatesta (1990)	Pa.[b]	Negative CAR on press date and press date through introduction in House
Margotta (1991)	Pa.[b]	Negative CAR 3 days around legislative event
Szewczyk and Tsetsekos (1992)	Pa.[b]	Negative CAR over 6-month event period

Disgorgement Statute

Study	State(s)	Result
Karpoff and Malatesta (1990)	Pa.[b]	Negative CAR on press date and press date through introduction in House

(Table continues.)

63

TABLE 4–1 (continued)

Type of Statute	State	Effects on Stock Prices
Margotta (1991)	Pa.[b]	Negative CAR 3 days around legislative event
Szewczyk and Tsetsekos (1992)	Pa.[b]	Negative CAR over 6-month event period
Fair Price Statute		
Karpoff and Malatesta (1989)	Multiple statutes	No significant effect
Mahla (1991)	Multiple statutes	No significant effect
Romano (1987)	Conn.	No significant effect
Other-Constituency Statute		
Romano (forthcoming)	Multiple statutes	No significant effect
Ryngaert and Netter (1988)	Ohio[c]	Negative CAR 2–10 days around legislative event
Margotta, McWilliams, and McWilliams (1990)	Ohio[c]	No significant effect over longer interval than that examined in Ryngaert and Netter study
Karpoff and Malatesta (1990)	Pa.[b]	Negative CAR on press date and press date through introduction in House
Margotta (1991)	Pa.[b]	Negative CAR 3 days around legislative event
Szewczyk and Tsetsekos (1992)	Pa.[b]	Negative CAR over 6-month event period

64

Poison pill statute		
Karpoff and Malatesta (1989)	Multiple statutes	Negative CAR over 2-day press date event interval
Ryngaert and Netter (1988)	Ohio[c]	Negative CAR 2–10 days around legislative event
Margotta, McWilliams, and McWilliams (1990)	Ohio[c]	No significant effect over longer interval than that examined in Ryngaert and Netter study
Redemption Rights Statute		
Schumann (1988)	N.Y.[a]	Negative CAR over 88-day interval up to governor's veto date; positive CAR significant at .06 over 3-day interval around veto
Pugh and Jahera (1990)	N.Y.[a]	Negative CAR on passage by second chamber
Romano (1987)	Pa.	No significant effect

AR = average residual.
CAR = cumulative average residual.
a. New York's first takeover statute, which was vetoed by the governor, includes a control share acquisition and a redemption rights provision.
b. Pennsylvania's takeover statute includes a control share acquisition, disgorgement, labor protection, and other-constituency provision.
c. Ohio's takeover statute includes an other-constituency and poison pill provision.

(Table continues.)

TABLE 4–1 (continued)

SOURCES: Jonathan Karpoff and Paul Malatesta, "The Wealth Effects of Second-Generation State Takeover Legislation," *Journal of Financial Economics*, vol. 25 (1989); Charles R. Mahla, Jr., *State Takeover Statutes and Shareholder Wealth* (Ph.D. diss., University of North Carolina, 1991); William N. Pugh and John S. Jahera, "State Antitakeover Legislation and Shareholder Wealth," *Journal of Financial Research*, vol. 13 (1990); John S. Jahera and William N. Pugh, "State Takeover Legislation: The Case of Delaware," *Journal of Law, Economics, and Organization*, vol. 7 (1991); Adam Broner, *New Jersey Shareholders Protection Act: An Economic Evaluation, A Report to the New Jersey Legislature* (Trenton, N.J.: Office of Economic Policy, State of New Jersey, 1987); Donald G. Margotta and Swaminathan Badrinath, "Effects of New Jersey Shareholder Protection Legislation on Stock Prices" (unpublished manuscript, 1987); Laurence Schumann, "State Regulation of Takeovers and Shareholder Wealth: The Effects of New York's 1985 Takeover Statutes," *RAND Journal of Economics*, vol. 19 (1988); Gregory Sidak and Susan Woodward, "Corporate Takeovers, the Commerce Clause, and the Efficient Anonymity of Shareholders," *Northwestern University Law Review*, vol. 84 (1990); Roberta Romano, "The Political Economy of Takeover Statutes," *Virginia Law Review*, vol. 73 (1987); Jonathan Karpoff and Paul Malatesta, "PA: State Antitakeover Laws and Stock Prices," *Financial Analysts Journal*, vol. 46 (July–August 1990); Donald G. Margotta, "Stock Price Effects of Pennsylvania Act 36" (unpublished manuscript, 1991); Samuel H. Szewczyk and George P. Tsetsekos, "State Intervention in the Market for Corporate Control: The Case of Pennsylvania Senate Bill 1310," *Journal of Financial Economics*, vol. 31 (1992); Roberta Romano, "What Is the Value of Other Constituency Statutes to Shareholders?" *University of Toronto Law Journal*, vol. 67 (forthcoming); Michael Ryngaert and Jeffry Netter, "Shareholder Wealth Effects of the Ohio Antitakeover Law," *Journal of Law, Economics, and Organization*, vol. 4 (1988); and Donald G. Margotta, Thomas P. McWilliams, and Victoria B. McWilliams, "An Analysis of the Stock Price Effect of the 1986 Ohio Takeover Legislation," *Journal of Law, Economics, and Organization*, vol. 6 (1990).

sample is broken down by type of takeover statute, the abnormal returns have a negative sign for control share acquisition, fair price, and business combination freeze provisions, but only the business combination freeze statutes' negative returns are statistically significant.[20] Finally, when the data are examined over time, only statutes enacted in 1986 or later have a significant negative price effect.[21]

Event studies of Delaware's second-generation statute find no significant stock price effect.[22] This datum is consistent with viewing Delaware's efforts at regulating takeovers as less restrictive than those of other states. Takeover statutes are thus a fascinating 180-degree role reversal of the Cary scenario of state competition. Delaware is more a reluctant follower than a leader, seeking to maintain its dominant market share, while other states race for the bottom to entrench management.[23] Whatever the adverse effect of state competition in regulating takeovers, Delaware is not the source of the problem.

Quite apart from Delaware's steady legislative policy of sailing against the wind when it comes to takeover regulation, California, a major corporate domicile, has still not adopted any takeover regulation. Thus, as not all states regulate takeovers, the relative values of

---

20. Ibid., pp. 312–13. The average abnormal returns across the three types of statutes do not, however, differ significantly.

21. This is not surprising as statutes enacted before 1986 and hence before *CTS* may well have been assumed to be unconstitutional under *MITE*. It is unfortunate that Karpoff and Malatesta took 1986 as the year for dividing their sample, because a more appropriate breakdown to capture the change in legal uncertainty is the year of the *CTS* decision, 1987; presumably, the number of observations in the subsamples dictated this choice, as their sample ended in 1987. Despite the constitutional uncertainty, the 1986 Indiana statute that was upheld in *CTS* had a significant negative impact on its enactment; Sidak and Woodward, "Corporate Takeovers, the Commerce Clause and the Efficient Anonymity of Shareholders." In another study of multiple statutes, however, Mahla finds that firms expect significant negative returns under statutes adopted before the *CTS* decision and not after it; Mahla, *State Takeover Statutes*, p. 109.

22. Jahera and Pugh, "State Takeover Legislation: The Case of Delaware"; Karpoff and Malatesta, "Wealth Effects of Second-Generation State Takeover Legislation," p. 315.

23. Mark J. Roe, "Takeover Politics," Brookings Discussion Paper in Economics 91-4 (Washington, D.C., 1991), pp. 52–53.

firms will be affected by remaining in a less valued (that is, more regulated) regime.[24]

Pennsylvania's disgorgement statute provides, paradoxically, a good example of the beneficent effect of state competition. Event studies of Pennsylvania firms have identified large significant negative abnormal returns at the time the legislation was enacted.[25] Institutional investors threatened to sell their shares in firms covered by the statute, and a majority of corporations opted out of the statute.[26] Of publicly traded firms with a Pennsylvania domicile whose choices were identified, as detailed in table 4–2 127 firms opted out of all or part of the statute, while 72 firms did not.[27] The proportion opting out is higher among larger firms (which are firms more likely to have a higher proportion of institutional investors): 32 firms listed on the New York Stock Exchange opted out and 11 did not. In fact, exchange-listed firms that opted out have a higher proportion of institutional owners than those that did not.[28] These data indicate that when a corporation's investors express concern about the impact of a particular corporation statute on their firm, managers will be responsive to their concerns. Researchers have further found that firms experience positive abnormal returns on opting out of the statute.[29]

---

24. See also Easterbrook and Fischel, *Economic Structure of Corporate Law*, p. 223.

25. For example, Szewczyk and Tsetsekos, "State Intervention in the Market for Corporate Control." For a review of several studies of this statute, which all report similar results, see M. Wayne Marr, "Survey of Empirical Studies: Pennsylvania Act 36," *Financial Analysts Journal*, vol. 48 (1992), p. 52.

26. See Leslie Wayne, "Many Companies in Pennsylvania Reject State's Takeover Protection," *New York Times* (July 20, 1990), p. 1. Firms were permitted to opt out of the statute by board approval (by amending corporate bylaws) within ninety days of the effective date.

27. I would like to thank the many Pennsylvania firms whose counsel provided me with information about their firm's choice and Robert Daines, who provided assistance in compiling this information.

28. Szewczyk and Tsetsekos, "State Intervention in the Market for Corporate Control," p. 18.

29. Ibid.; Marr, "Survey of Empirical Studies: Pennsylvania's Act 36." The full sample of firms opting out of all or some of the provisions and the subsample of firms opting out of all provisions experience significant positive abnormal returns,

TABLE 4–2
FIRM CHOICES ON COVERAGE OF PENNSYLVANIA'S
1990 TAKEOVER STATUTE

Choice	Exchange Firms[a]	Other Firms[b]	Total
Opting out of entire statute	18	33	51
Opting out of control share acquisition[c], disgorgement, and other constituency provisions	0	2	2
Opting out of control share acquisition[c] and disgorgement provisions	21	39	60
Opting out of control share acquisition[c] and other-constituency provisions	0	1	1
Opting out of disgorgement and other-constituency provisions	0	1	1
Opting out of disgorgement provision only	3	0	3
Opting out of control share acquisition provision[c] only	1	8	9
Not opting out of statute	15	57	72
Unidentified	5	104	109
Total	63	245	308

a. These Pennsylvania firms are listed on New York Stock Exchange or American Stock Exchange.
b. These Pennsylvania firms are listed on other exchanges, the National Market Service of the National Association of Securities Dealers, or traded over the counter.
c. Opting out of control share acquisition provision automatically opts firm out of labor protection provisions as well.
SOURCE: Author's survey of Pennsylvania firms, conducted for this monograph.

The widespread withdrawal by Pennsylvania firms from inclusion under a value-decreasing statute powerfully supports the acuity of

but the abnormal return for the subset of firms that only partially opt out is insignificant.

Winter's critique of Cary. Capital markets discipline managers, notwithstanding their best efforts at entrenchment, by placing a floor on deleterious state competition. Additional confirmation of this contention, besides the large number of firms opting out of coverage, is the fact that, in contrast to other innovations in takeover regulation, few states have followed Pennsylvania's lead and enacted a disgorgement provision.[30]

The centrality of takeover statutes in defeating bids—and, correspondingly, in assessing the desirability of state competition for corporate charters—can be easily overestimated. Some commentators contend that the lull in activity in hostile takeovers in the late 1980s and early 1990s is largely due to the effect of second- and third-generation takeover statutes.[31] Such an analysis predicts that takeover statutes should have a pronounced negative stock price effect, but event studies do not identify such a large impact. While the data indicate that takeover statutes decrease investor wealth, the magnitude of the decline is small. Indeed, one study concludes that credit restrictions, and not takeover statutes, account for the decline in takeovers.[32] Moreover, managers are able to thwart takeover bids without statutory assistance by using a variety of defensive tactics.

In particular, poison pills, shark repellent charter amendments, and dual-class voting structures are potent substitutes for takeover statutes.[33] Event studies of defensive tactics find significant negative

---

30. According to the Investor Responsibility Research Center, only one other state, Ohio, has copied Pennsylvania's disgorgement provision. IRRC, *State Takeover Laws* (Washington, D.C.: IRRC, updated through summer 1991).

31. For example, Roe, "Takeover Politics."

32. Robert Comment and G. William Schwert, "Poison or Placebo? Evidence on the Deterrent and Wealth Effects of Modern Antitakeover Measures" (unpublished manuscript, University of Rochester Graduate School of Business Administration, 1993).

33. Poison pills are shareholder rights plans in which firms issue warrants on the common stock giving the holder the right to acquire preferred stock for a low price if the firm is subject to a tender offer or a block of common stock is accumulated, without board approval. The terms of the preferred stock greatly increase the bidder's acquisition costs. For a general discussion and critique of these plans, see Jeffrey MacIntosh, "The Poison Pill: A Noxious Nostrum for Canadian Shareholders," *Canadian Business Law Journal*, vol. 15 (1989), p. 276. Defensive charter amendments, which are called shark repellents, come in many varieties, including supermajority voting requirements to approve business combinations with interested

returns on their adoption of the same magnitude as, or higher than, that found by Karpoff and Malatesta for takeover statutes.[34] In addition, Karpoff and Malatesta found that the stock price effect of takeover laws is significantly negative for firms without poison pill and charter defenses and insignificant for firms with such defenses, but such a substitution effect has not been uncovered in all studies.[35]

---

parties, fair price requirements for second-step mergers occurring after successful tender offers, staggered boards, and elimination of cumulative voting rights. For a critique of such provisions, see Ronald J. Gilson, "The Case against Shark Repellent Amendments: Structural Limitations on the Enabling Concept," *Stanford Law Review,* vol. 34 (1982), p. 775. Dual-class stock refers to firms with two classes of voting stock, one with low or no voting rights and the other with high or all voting rights; public investors hold the former, and insiders hold the latter shares. This contrasts with the corporate voting norm of one share—one vote and removes the firm from the market for corporate control, as a bidder could not acquire sufficient shares to wrest control from the insiders. Most firms adopting such voting structures, however, were already controlled by insiders and hence not subject to takeover; the change simply consolidated that control. For a thorough critique of such voting structures, see Jeffrey N. Gordon, "Ties That Bond: Dual Class Common Stock and the Problem of Shareholder Choice," *California Law Review,* vol. 76 (1988), p. 2.

34. See, for example, Paul H. Malatesta and Ralph A. Walkling, "Poison Pill Securities: Stockholder Wealth, Profitability, and Ownership Structure," *Journal of Financial Economics,* vol. 20 (1988), p. 347 (− 0.34 percent abnormal return for pill adoptions reported in the press; − 0.17 percent for all pill adoptions); Michael Ryngaert, "The Effect of Poison Pill Securities on Shareholder Wealth," *Journal of Financial Economics,* vol. 20 (1988), p. 377 (− 0.3 percent abnormal return); Sanjai Bhagat and James Brickley, "The Value of Minority Shareholder Voting Rights," *Journal of Law and Economics,* vol. 27 (1984), p. 339 (− 1 percent abnormal return on elimination of cumulative voting rights); Gregg A. Jarrell and Annette B. Poulsen, "Shark Repellents and Stock Prices: The Effects of Anti-takeover Amendments since 1980," *Journal of Financial Economics,* vol. 19 (1987), p. 127 (− 3 percent abnormal returns to supermajority amendments but insignificant − 0.7 percent abnormal returns to fair price amendments).

35. Karpoff and Malatesta, "Wealth Effects of Second-Generation State Takeover Legislation," pp. 311–12; see also Szewczyk and Tsetsekos, "State Intervention in the Market for Corporate Control," p. 15 (significant difference). This result is supportive of the thesis that firms whose managers fear they would not obtain shareholder approval of defensive tactics are most desirous of legislation. Pugh and Jahera, however, did not find a similar pattern of returns to firms with and without defensive charter amendments in four of five states they examined. But they also did not find negative effects of the statutes on the full sample of firms, and they did not control for poison pill plans, which are the more potent defense; Pugh and Jahera, "State Antitakeover Legislation and Shareholder Wealth"; Jahera and Pugh,

These data corroborate managers' and practitioners' contentions that poison pills, and not takeover statutes, are the principal defense to unwanted bids.[36] They are also inconsistent with viewing the lull in takeover activity as caused by state takeover legislation, because they suggest that investors consider statutes less harmful to their interests than defensive tactics.[37]

The finding that takeover statutes are less effective than, and perhaps even a substitute for, defensive tactics underscores another important facet of state competition. The use of defensive tactics is as much a part of state competition as statutory enactments because management's strategies that are not subject to shareholder approval, such as poison pills, are reviewed by courts. Indeed, some legislatures have used takeover statutes to restrain courts from safeguarding shareholders' investments, a strategy that is at odds with a positive assessment of state competition. Here again, Delaware's judiciary, which as discussed plays an important role in Delaware's success in the charter market, is a moderating influence. The Delaware courts have not one-sidedly favored incumbent managers, for they have invalidated defensive maneuvers and forced poison pill redemptions.[38]

"State Takeover Legislation: The Case of Delaware." Similarly, Romano finds no evidence of a substitution effect from other constituency statutes: firms without poison pill defenses experienced insignificant positive abnormal returns, and those with defenses experienced insignificant negative returns; Romano, "Value of Other Constituency Statutes."

36. For example, this view was emphatically articulated by Charles Exley, NCR's incumbent chief executive officer who failed to fend off American Telephone & Telegraph's unwanted bid, in remarks at the ABA's National Institute on Dynamics of Corporate Control (New York, December 5, 1991), and by Thomas G. Cody, senior vice president for law and public affairs of Federated Department Stores, which eventually capitulated to Campeau Corporation's hostile bid, in remarks at the *University of Cincinnati Law Review* and College of Law Conference on Regulating Corporate Takeovers (Cincinnati, April 15, 1988).

37. To the extent that regulatory and not economic conditions contributed to the lull, it is most likely a function of restricted financing opportunities, with the collapse of the junk bond market, caused by congressional restrictions on financial institutions' high-yield debt holdings and participation in highly leveraged transactions. For support of this view, see Comment and Schwert, "Poison or Placebo?"

38. Well-known cases invalidating defensive tactics include Revlon, Inc. v. MacAndrews & Forbes Holdings, 506 A.2d 173 (Del. 1986) and Capital City Associates Limited Partners v. Interco, 551 A.2d 787 (Del.Ch. 1988).

The most recent important Delaware decision before the lull in takeover activity was *Paramount Communications v. Time Inc.*,[39] in which the court upheld Time management's restructuring of a merger with Warner Brothers solely to avoid a Time shareholder vote because Paramount had made a tender offer for Time and management knew that the shareholders would vote against the merger to receive Paramount's much higher premium. The decision has led some commentators to suggest that Delaware has capitulated and joined the race to the bottom, although other commentators strenuously disagree.[40] It is too soon to tell whether *Paramount* is a significant retrenchment by the Delaware court in protecting shareholder interests, for without seeing the standard's application we cannot determine how broad or narrow an understanding of its holding the court has in mind.

A favorable evaluation of Delaware courts in takeover disputes is supported by the reaction of other state legislatures. Because many state courts look to Delaware precedents for guidance, state legislatures have sought to reduce Delaware's impact in the takeover context (and only this context). The Indiana legislature, for example, in enacting takeover legislation expressly instructed its courts not to follow Delaware's approach, which it found too accommodating to bidders.[41] In addition, some legislatures have enacted statutes expressly upholding the use of poison pills, either to reverse specific decisions voiding pills or to respond to concern over the possible outcome of judicial review of pills in the absence of broad legislative authorization.[42]

Other-constituency statutes can also be viewed as an exercise in

---

39. 571 A.2d 1140 (Del. 1990).

40. Compare Roe, "Takeover Politics," with Fred S. McChesney and William J. Carney, "The Theft of Time, Inc.?: Efficient Law and Efficient Markets," *Regulation* (Spring 1991), p. 78. One commentator provides what he terms a sociohistorical account of the decision, as reflecting changed cultural and philosophical attitudes regarding the operation of markets; Jeffrey N. Gordon, "Corporations, Markets, and Courts," *Columbia Law Review*, vol. 91 (1991), p. 1931.

41. Ind. Stat. Ann. § 23-1-35-1(f) (West 1989 & Supp. 1990).

42. When courts require poison pills to be redeemed, the sued firms experience significant positive abnormal returns, but when courts reject demands for pill redemptions, the firms experience significant negative abnormal returns. See Ryngaert, "Effect of Poison Pill Securities on Shareholder Wealth."

legislative control of courts, for they instruct courts to permit directors the broadest discretion in resisting takeover bids.[43] These laws do not appear to have as harmful an impact on shareholders as other second-generation statutes. In an event study of other-constituency statutes, I found no significant stock price effects, whether or not firms had poison pill antitakeover defenses.[44] This insignificance signals that the statutes do not affect the law of takeovers. Namely, the market does not expect management's reaction to bids, or courts' evaluation of management's defensive behavior, to change under such statutes. If boards already factor in stakeholders' interests when engaging in defensive tactics with judicial approval, then enactment of other-constituency statutes will have no impact on investor wealth. This explanation is plausible, because most statutes have been added to codes already replete with antitakeover provisions, and the statutes do not provide stakeholders with the right to take legal action against the board to ensure that their interests are properly considered.[45] But consistent with a scenario of efficacious state competition, Delaware has not enacted an other-constituency statute, and Delaware courts permit the interests of other constituents to be considered only if there are "rationally related benefits accruing to the shareholders."[46]

Proxy contests for the election of the board provide an alternative change of control mechanism to takeovers. Although proxy fights were common in the nineteenth and early twentieth centuries, they have become less frequent than takeovers since the 1960s. John Pound suggested that proxy fights became more expensive compared with takeovers because of increased regulation of proxies by the SEC during the mid-1950s.[47] With the onslaught of state takeover regula-

---

43. For a discussion of the relation between these statutes and the common law, which concludes that, for the most part, the statutes will not have a significant impact on corporate governance compared to what courts would decide without legislation, see Charles Hansen, "Other Constituency Statutes: A Search for Perspective," *Business Lawyer,* vol. 46 (1991), p. 1355.

44. Romano, "Value of Other Constituency Statutes."

45. Ibid.

46. Hansen, "Other Constituency Statutes," p. 1364.

47. John Pound, "Proxy Voting and the SEC," *Journal of Financial Economics,* vol. 29 (1991), p. 241. The absolute costs of takeovers also declined with the advent of new financing techniques in the 1980s.

tion, the cost differential has been reduced, and for a brief time in the early 1990s, it appeared that the number of proxy contests would rise to compensate for the decline in takeover activity. In response, a few states made takeover statutes—control share acquisition and disgorgement provisions—applicable to proxy contests as well. But the number of proxy fights did not accelerate as expected, and, correspondingly, states were not pressed to further restrict proxy contests. If mergers and acquisitions occur in waves,[48] however, the decline in proxy contests for control would be due to the same economic phenomena that induced the end of the recent swell in takeovers. Accordingly, the number of proxy fights may well rise relative to that of takeovers in the next acquisition wave; without doubt, that will inspire greater state regulation.

Should Takeover Regulation Be Nationalized?

Delaware stands out from the pack, whether its corporation code or case law on takeovers is examined. Still, it is plausible to maintain that Delaware would not have enacted any takeover legislation in the absence of state competition.[49] Acknowledging that the track record of most states in takeover regulation raises serious questions concerning the efficacy of state competition does not imply that national regulation of takeovers is the solution to an imperfect federal system. This is just the beginning of the inquiry. The principal analytical problem in advocating national control is that while everyone affected by the regulation will now reside in the legislating jurisdiction, the beneficiaries—corporate managers—are still a concentrated group, and those bearing the costs—shareholders—are still diffuse.

Problems of collective action involving asymmetric organizational advantages of managers over shareholders are not avoided at the national level. Managers are still more easily organized across firms than shareholders, regardless of the forum. Business trade

---

48. See Devra L. Golbe and Lawrence J. White, "Mergers and Acquisitions in the U.S. Economy: An Aggregate and Historical Overview," in A. Auerbach, ed., *Mergers and Acquisitions* (Chicago: University of Chicago Press, 1988), p. 25. The view that mergers occur in waves is disputed by some economists. See, for example, William F. Shughart II and Robert D. Tollison, "The Random Character of Merger Activity," *RAND Journal of Economics*, vol. 15 (1984), p. 500.

49. See Roe, "Takeover Politics."

organizations, such as chambers of commerce, provide valuable information to their members, inducing individual participation in collective action.[50] Shareholder organizations are at a comparative disadvantage, as they provide individuals with far fewer inducements to action. In recent years, however, institutional investors have begun to organize and engage in lobbying activities, no doubt in reaction to efforts by state legislatures to expropriate their wealth. Further, individuals are more likely to coordinate their actions to avoid losses than to achieve gains because of risk aversion (they care more about preventing losses than achieving gains of equal magnitude).[51] This attitude, again, favors incumbent managers, who stand to lose from takeovers compared with shareholders. Finally, the cost-benefit calculus is not changed when moving from state to national level: the average top manager's financial interest in the outcome of a takeover is much greater than the average shareholder's, and management's lobbying expenditures are paid by the corporation.

While the national political dynamic still favors managers, the congressional output might differ from that of the states. The record to date, however, is that in the takeover area Congress mimics the states. The impetus for congressional action on takeovers, which in the 1980s consisted primarily of hearings and introduction of bills, rather than the enactment of securities legislation, and the addition of tax provisions directed at increasing the cost of takeovers, is the same as that of states: a hostile bid for a major firm located in the sponsoring legislators' state.[52] Moreover, as table 4–3 makes clear,

---

50. For a discussion of the theoretical literature on collective action and its relation to the organization of managers versus shareholders, see Romano, "Future of Hostile Takeovers," pp. 468–70.

51. Russell Hardin, *Collective Action* (Baltimore: Johns Hopkins University Press, 1982), pp. 83, 120–21; Romano, "Future of Hostile Takeovers," p. 470.

52. Romano, "Future of Hostile Takeovers," pp. 482–84 (detailing examples). There is a significant correlation between the sponsors of federal takeover legislation and the location of a hostile bid target in their district; Kenneth Lehn and James W. Jones, "The Legislative Politics of Hostile Corporate Takeovers" (unpublished manuscript, Washington University, 1987). The states are able to act more quickly than Congress. The federal tax legislation on takeovers during the 1980s consisted of the imposition of penalty excise taxes on payments of greenmail and golden parachutes, restriction of the use of net operating losses in acquisitions, and repeal

TABLE 4-3
WITNESSES AT CONGRESSIONAL HEARINGS ON TAKEOVER LEGISLATION,
1963–1987

| | Hearings[a] | |
Witness	Number	Percent
Federal government[b]	62	81
Target management	46	60
Academic	37	48
Member of congress	32	42
State or local government	23	30
Labor union	19	25
Takeover bidder	15	20
Investment bank	15	20
Stock exchange	4	5
Shareholder organization	2	3

a. Of seventy-seven hearings on takeover-related legislation or particular bids, held from 1963 to 1987, number and percent with at least one witness of specified type.
b. Executive branch or agency official or employee.
SOURCE: Roberta Romano, "The Future of Hostile Takeovers: Legislation and Public Opinion," *University of Cincinnati Law Review*, vol. 57 (1988), pp. 457, 485.

the principal witnesses at congressional hearings are corporate managers and government employees or elected officials; labor groups are rarely witnesses, and shareholders are rarer still.[53] More important, the vast majority of the bills introduced in Congress rival the states in efforts at restricting bids.[54]

---

of the provision permitting corporate distributions of appreciated property without payment of the corporate-level tax. For an analysis indicating that managers won the day in the two excise tax reforms, see Romano, "Guide to Takeovers" (suggesting that the only tactics Congress chose to restrict were those likely to benefit shareholders by facilitating bids), which is summarized hereafter. For a critique of the latter two reforms, see Roberta Romano, "Rethinking Takeover Regulation," *Journal of Applied Corporate Finance* (Fall 1992), p. 47.

53. Romano, "Future of Hostile Takeovers," p. 485.

54. Ibid., p. 472.

Table 4–4 provides a breakdown of the content of all bills introduced in Congress from the passage of the Williams Act in 1969 through the *CTS* decision in 1987.[55] The principal approaches for regulating takeovers in the bills are (1) to delay the consummation of bids by extending waiting periods for bid completion or government approval, requiring additional federal agency approval or review if an acquisition will result in layoffs; (2) to increase acquisition costs by closing the ten-day window before an ownership disclosure filing must be made under section 13(d) of the Williams Act, lowering the threshold ownership for such disclosure below the current 5 percent, increasing disclosure obligations, prohibiting purchases of control blocks or two-tier or partial takeovers unless made as tender offers to all shareholders, and prohibiting banks from financing takeovers or purchasing the high-yield bonds issued in takeovers; and (3) to ban some or all takeovers (for example, bans on noncash tender offers, hostile offers, highly leveraged hostile offers, takeovers by foreign investors, or all acquisitions in certain industries). Several bills proposed a national control-share acquisition statute, others expressly protected state regulation from preemption, and one would have reversed an SEC regulation prohibiting the defensive tactic known as a selective self-tender, in which incumbent management makes a tender offer that excludes the bidder's shares from participation.

Some bills also restrict defensive tactics. This is not clear-cut evidence of a more balanced political process than that of state legislatures, because the regulated tactics—golden parachutes and greenmail—are ones that commentators on corporate law believe most likely to benefit shareholders and to encourage bids. Golden parachutes, for example, better align managers' interest with shareholders, making resistance to a bid less likely, because they will be compensated if the new owner replaces them.[56] Greenmail may also

---

55. A total of 199 bills were identified from the subject index of the Commerce Clearing House's *Congressional Index* 91st to 100th Congresses (Chicago: CCH, 1969–1987). Bills regulating acquisitions of banks were excluded from the tally, because they implicate special regulatory issues requiring reform of existing federal banking regulation under the Glass-Steagall Act.

56. For example, David Baron, "Tender Offers and Management Resistance," *Journal of Finance*, vol. 38 (1983), p. 331. The stock price effect of golden parachutes is positive, although this finding could be caused by a signaling effect,

TABLE 4–4
Congressional Bills Regulating Takeovers, 1969–1987

Type of Bill	Number of Bills
By General Category[a]	
Regulation of bidders only	48
Regulation of defensive tactics only	4
Regulation of both bidders and defensive tactics	22
Regulation of acquisitions in energy, transportation, and communications industries	48
Regulation of acquisitions by foreigners	51
Taxation of acquisitions	26
Total	199
By Specific Proposal[b]	
Extension of time period of bid	15
Lower ownership threshold and closing of 10-day window for disclosure under § 13(d) of the Williams Act	18
Community impact statement requirement	10
Prohibition on control block purchases, two-tier offers, and partial offers	12
Prohibition of hostile acquisitions	5
Restrictions on high-yield bond purchases by banks	8
Control share acquisition statute	7
Restrictions on greenmail	19
Restrictions on golden parachutes	10
Restrictions on dual-class voting stock	4
Denial of interest deduction for acquisition debt	16
Repeal of the Williams Act	1
Total	125

a. Bills involving acquisitions of banks are excluded, because they implicate special regulatory issues requiring reform of federal banking regulation established by the Glass-Steagall Act.

b. Specific proposal counts overlap: for example, a bill that extends the time period for a bid, lowers the disclosure threshold under section 13(d) and includes restrictions on greenmail would be counted as a bill in all three categories.

SOURCE: Commerce Clearing House, *Congressional Index*, 91st to 100th Congresses (Chicago: CCH, 1969–1987).

maximize shareholder wealth by inducing a second and higher bidder, which does not want to engage in an auction, to acquire the firm.[57] Tactics considered most likely to defeat bids and therefore to diminish shareholder wealth, such as poison pills, however, are not the subject of congressional interest.[58]

The overwhelmingly one-sided (antibidder) aspect of bills that have persistently been on Congress's agenda over the years regarding takeovers is significant, because successful law reform is typically a recombination of old elements already in the legislative hopper rather than a completely new proposal.[59] Moreover, the Williams Act itself was not neutral regulation: it tilted the playing field toward incumbent management over bidders.[60]

---

that the adoption indicates that management thinks a takeover attempt, with its higher stock price, is likely, rather than to investors' evaluation of a parachute's effect on management's behavior. See Richard Lambert and Donald Larckner, "Golden Parachutes, Executive Decision-making and Shareholder Wealth," *Journal of Accounting and Economics*, vol. 7 (1985), p. 179.

57. For example, Jonathan Macey and Fred McChesney, "A Theoretical Analysis of Greenmail," *Yale Law Journal*, vol. 95 (1985), p. 13; Andrei Shleifer and Robert W. Vishny, "Greenmail, White Knights, and Shareholders' Interest," *RAND Journal of Economics*, vol. 17 (1986), p. 293. The stock price effect of greenmail payments is negative, but the cumulative effect from the greenmailer's initial stock purchase through the corporation's repurchase of its shares is positive. See Wayne H. Mikkelson and Richard S. Ruback, "Targeted Repurchases and Common Stock Returns," *RAND Journal of Economics*, vol. 22 (1991), p. 544; Clifford G. Holderness and Dennis P. Sheehan, "Raiders or Saviors? The Evidence on Six Controversial Investors," *Journal of Financial Economics*, vol. 14 (1985), p. 555; Office of the Chief Economist, Securities and Exchange Commission, "The Impact of Targetted Share Repurchases (Greenmail) on Stock Prices" (Washington, D.C.: 1984). In addition, 29 percent of firms paying greenmail experience control changes within three years of the payment. See Mikkelson and Ruback, supra.

58. In contrast to golden parachutes and greenmail, the stock price effects of defensive tactics like poison pills are negative. See Ryngaert, "The Effect of Poison Pill Securities on Shareholder Wealth"; Malatesta and Walkling, "Poison Pill Securities, Shareholder Wealth, Profitability and Ownership Structure."

59. John Kingdon, *Agendas, Alternatives and Public Policies* (Boston: Little, Brown and Company, 1984), p. 131. In fact, the major federal takeover legislation, such as the Williams Act and the Hart-Scott-Rodino Antitrust Improvements Act of 1976, 15 U.S.C. § 18a, requiring prenotification and a waiting period for mergers involving large firms, had been contained in bills introduced over several previous sessions.

60. See Easterbrook and Fischel, *Economic Structure of Corporate Law*, pp. 224–

Despite a heightened level of congressional interest, no major substantive takeover statute was enacted in the 1980s, in large part because the Reagan and Bush administrations opposed increased regulation. Lacking agency and presidential support, Congress had little incentive to legislate, for it was confronted with either a veto fight or an uncooperative agency that could thwart legislative objectives by unenthusiastic implementation. In addition, the Supreme Court's *CTS* decision reduced the pressure on Congress to act, as target managers could concentrate their appeals for relief on state legislatures, which had already shown themselves to be highly cooperative. Indeed, state legislatures were capable of acting far more quickly than Congress, which during the 1980s would hardly finish the hearings stage in the legislative process before a protective state takeover statute was enacted or a bid completed.

National mood is another important variable in policy agenda formation,[61] and the public, while largely ignorant of the economic effects of takeovers, has an unfavorable opinion of the transactions.[62] Examples of the public's consistently negative, yet uninformed, opinion of takeovers are the views that (1) workers are the losers and acquiring firm shareholders and executives the winners in takeovers, and (2) mergers are bad for the economy.[63] A massive literature on acquisitions, however, points precisely in the opposite direction: as noted, the only systematic losers in takeovers are top or middle-level management, not production workers.[64] Moreover, it is target, not acquiring firm, shareholders who gain from the transactions.[65] Finally, the bulk of the evidence indicates that the sources of takeover gains are efficiency-enhancing improvements in firm operations and not wealth transfers from one group of firm participants to shareholders.[66]

---

25. This is also true of the Hart-Scott-Rodino Act, for prebid disclosure exacerbates the problems for bidders from delay in a bid's completion discussed earlier in the text.

61. Kingdon, *Agendas, Alternatives, and Public Policies.*

62. See Romano, "Future of Hostile Takeovers," pp. 490–502.

63. Ibid.

64. See Romano, "Guide to Takeovers."

65. Ibid.

66. Ibid.

Social psychologists have found that the subjective availability of information about an event affects judgments of causality. This finding may explain the persistence of the public's inaccurate impressions of takeovers. People tend to be influenced by the accessibility of an event in their cognitive processes, even though there is no correlation between this accessibility and the objective probability of the event.[67] A news story on a takeover resulting in unemployed workers will, in this view, be vividly remembered and considered evidence of the negative effects of acquisitions, while numerous other accounts of acquisitions without job losses will not disconfirm the initial news account because they are not dramatic enough to register with the observer.[68]

The combination of a poorly informed public, which tends to question the value of takeovers, and managers' organizational advantages in lobbying creates little political benefit for national legislators to act differently from state legislators when it comes to regulating takeovers. As a consequence, further national legislation is unlikely to be more hospitable to the market for corporate control than state legislation. A leading publication for institutional investors reached a similar conclusion. In an editorial responding to the enactment of the 1990 Pennsylvania takeover statute, *Pensions and Investments Age* wrote: "Some leaders in the investment community suggest looking to Congress to head off the states. But federal representatives succumb to the same temptations as state legislators."[69]

The recent history of state takeover laws does not weaken the case for state corporation law advanced in earlier chapters but, to the contrary, is one more example of the merits of state competition. As the Pennsylvania experience illustrates, the federal system provides a safety net against the consequences of harmful state laws. Some jurisdictions will have no or only mild takeover regulation, and this constrains how much other jurisdictions can act in this area and how much firms can take advantage of value-decreasing laws, especially when major commercial states such as Delaware and California have

---

67. See Richard Nisbett and Lee Ross, *Human Inference: Strategies and Shortcomings of Social Judgment* (Englewood Cliffs, N.J.: Prentice-Hall, 1980), pp. 18–19.

68. Ibid., pp. 21–22.

69. "Demand Liberty, or Sell," *Pensions and Investment Age* (April 30, 1990), p. 16.

less onerous laws. Such a restraining mechanism is not present at the national level, yet members of Congress experience the same demands as state legislatures to tilt the regulatory apparatus toward management. There is nothing to suggest that given the opportunity they would not do so. In addition, the diversity of laws of fifty states on controversial subjects such as takeovers produces a continuous flow of information concerning the effect of different policy choices (such as the event studies discussed in this chapter), which would be curtailed under a uniform national approach.

These considerations counsel against championing national intervention. Calling for national legislation with the expectation of reversing state restrictions of takeovers[70] is wishful thinking at best and could well be counterproductive, because it will in all probability produce even more damaging legislation. While the downside of the state system would remain with such national legislation, federalism's upside potential, protection against poor policy choices, would be absent. At a minimum, commentators who seek preemption of state takeover laws first must better inform the public about how the market for corporate control works for their benefit.[71] For without popular support, Congress is unlikely to cross the organized and politically well-connected opponents of hostile takeovers.

Can we do better than the existing regulatory regime for takeovers? The optimal policy would be repeal of laws that have been found to affect stock prices adversely—control share acquisition and business combination freeze statutes. But the likelihood of this occurring, given present political realities, is low. The second best policy would be for states to adopt the politically more palatable reform of making it easier for firms to opt out of a takeover statute, which would provide shareholders with a more meaningful choice

---

70. See, for example, Roe, "Takeover Politics."

71. Morey McDaniel, in criticizing my thesis, asserts that the public is concerned about losers and not winners from takeovers, Morey W. McDaniel, "Stockholders and Stakeholders," *Stetson Law Review*, vol. 21 (1991), pp. 121, 154 n. 120. This contention misses my point: there is a vast amount of misinformation being peddled to the public by corporate managers about alleged victims of hostile takeovers, but there is *no* systematic evidence that these takeovers harm workers, although there is considerable evidence that top managers—who are the principal publicists concerning the evils of hostile takeovers—often do lose their jobs. See Romano, "Guide to Takeovers."

concerning takeover regulation. In particular, statutory defaults ought to be changed from opt-out to opt-in regimes, following the legislative practice of Georgia.

The conventional approach to statutory defaults is to choose what the majority of firms would adopt, if they had to specify a provision in their charters. Such a default permits firms to avoid the transaction costs of holding a shareholder vote when approval would be pro forma. The negative stock price effects from the enactment of takeover statutes suggest that the conventional scenario does not apply to takeover statutes, because shareholders presumably would not choose to be governed by a provision that adversely affects their wealth. Indeed, since most restrictions imposed by second-generation statutes can be adopted voluntarily by charter amendment without an authorizing statute, management's lobbying for legislation clearly implies that it believes it easier to convince a state legislature than shareholders of an antitakeover provision's desirability. Reform of statutory defaults to require shareholder approval at least guarantees that the decision to reduce stock prices is put into the hands of those who bear the financial consequences. It is also politically feasible: it reframes the discussion into one of corporate voting, on which it is more difficult for legislators to oppose shareholders than on corporate takeovers, as shareholder voting rights will resonate more favorably with the public than shareholder rights to bid premiums. In addition, the lobbying of business organizations against such a change would emphasize that management is taking the legislative route in order to short-circuit shareholder voting out of a fear that the proposal would be rejected if presented for a vote. Such motivation is less visible when lobbying is over the substantive content of takeover regulation rather than the default for coverage. Yet once visible, it would not be accorded much weight in the legislative debate, as it strips shareholders of the right to vote, inverting the agency relation between owners and managers.

The optional feature of state takeover statutes is not a characteristic of the national regime. Limited experimentation, designed to discover the optimal regime, by enabling firms to opt out of the Williams Act or federal proxy contest regulation on a shareholder vote, would be desirable in the national context as well. Chapter 5 more closely examines this issue and the extent to which there should be mandatory corporate and securities laws.

5

The Enabling Structure
of Corporation Codes and
Mandatory Securities Laws

MODERN CORPORATION CODES tend to be enabling rather than mandatory statutes: they are standard form contracts specifying the rights and obligations of managers and shareholders, which can often be altered by private agreement to suit the circumstances of particular firms. The enabling approach is a function of the contractual nature of the corporation. Participation in a firm is voluntary; common stock is one of a vast array of available investment vehicles. Although an enabling regime permits shareholders and management to tailor most corporate contract terms to fit their particular needs, the appropriate scope of the regime—whether certain corporate code provisions should be mandatory rather than optional—is a perennial debate among students and practitioners of corporate law. State securities regulation, conversely, is mandatory when it applies. Its jurisdiction is based on the site of the securities transaction (that is, the state of residence of the citizen-purchaser) and not the issuer's domicile.

The mandatory-enabling debate can be recast to fit the theme of this monograph: does state competition produce too few mandatory corporate laws? Because of the ease of reincorporation, a provision in one state's code will not be truly mandatory unless it is included in all other state codes. This leads proponents of mandatory rules to advocate exclusive national corporate laws, which firms could circumvent only by resorting to costly substitutes such as adopting an unincorporated form of business or incorporating in a foreign country.

The case for a national corporation law to ensure mandatory compliance parallels the case for the federal securities laws, from

85

which corporations cannot opt out. An implicit assumption in the comparison is that the federal securities laws work well and ought to be emulated. When analyzed carefully, however, the rationales for the federal securities laws are quite weak, having little to do with shareholder protection, and the empirical evidence of their efficacy is, at best, inconclusive. There is no compelling reason for *mandating* federal laws governing the content and timing of disclosure of financial and other information, the conduct of tender offers, and trading on inside information. Yet if the strictures of the federal securities laws were enabling rather than mandatory, then the justification for having a national as opposed to state regime is removed. Hence, far from providing ammunition to opponents of state corporate chartering, an examination of the performance of the federal securities laws makes the case for a national corporation code even more problematic. Similarly, the experience with mandatory state securities laws does not support altering the enabling approach of state corporation codes. Despite the negative conclusions concerning the efficacy of the federal government's involvement in securities regulation, there has been a troubling expansion in recent years of its jurisdiction in the federal criminalization of fiduciary duties under the mail and wire fraud statutes.

Arguments in the Mandatory-Enabling Debate

Some commentators use arguments of imperfect information to advocate a substantial mandatory component in corporation codes. They contend that shareholders are inadequately informed about charter terms compared with manager-drafters and thus mistakenly invest in firms with disadvantageous charter terms, a situation that could be avoided by prohibiting the offending provisions.[1] More sophisticated analyses suggest that the problem is not asymmetrical information concerning firm quality before initial stock purchases but rather opportunistic behavior by managers that occurs midstream, after the public has already invested in a firm.[2] The assertion is that managers

---

1. For example, Melvin A. Eisenberg, "The Structure of Corporation Law," *Columbia Law Review*, vol. 89 (1989), pp. 1461, 1464–70.

2. For example, Jeffrey N. Gordon, "The Mandatory Structure of Corporate Law," *Columbia Law Review*, vol. 89 (1989), p. 1549.

propose value-decreasing charter amendments after equity investments are made, and, for a variety of reasons, investors are compelled
to approve these amendments. In this view, mandatory provisions are
desirable to precommit managers to eschew such a strategy. Typical
code provisions identified as rules from which firms should not be
permitted to opt out are the fiduciary duty of loyalty (which regulates
conflicts of interest) and voting rights.

The imperfect information argument for mandatory laws loses
force when we acknowledge that firms are situated in capital markets,
just as this recognition weakens Cary's position in the federalism
debate. An efficient market—one that quickly incorporates the value
of new information about a firm into stock prices—will price corporate charter terms, and hence investors will not bear the cost of
harmful terms adopted under enabling statutes in such markets: they
will get what they pay for. Moreover, in such a market, only some
investors need be informed about contract terms to ensure that they
are priced.[3] Initial offerings and secondary stock markets offer the
same price to all investors, and informed investors will not overpay
for value-decreasing charter provisions. The efficiency of U.S. capital
markets undermines the argument of initial contract information
asymmetry for mandatory rules but not necessarily the argument of
midstream opportunism. That contractual changes are priced when
proposed is little solace to shareholders who have already made their
investments. A mandatory rule preventing revision of initial contract
terms would therefore eliminate capital losses resulting from such
opportunism. If shareholders, however, anticipate future managerial
misconduct, the costs of midstream opportunism will be impounded
in the initial price. While the particular form of opportunism may
not be foreseen, the possibility of such conduct will be.

If initial shares are not properly discounted for future opportunism, shareholders and not managers will bear the cost of midstream
charter amendments. Under all state codes, however, shareholders
must approve charter amendments. The rationale of midstream opportunism for mandatory provisions would thus appear to be a non-
issue: why would shareholders vote for a provision that decreases
their wealth? The conventional response is that shareholders are

---

3. See, generally, Ronald Gilson and Reinier Kraakman, "The Mechanisms of
Market Efficiency," *Virginia Law Review*, vol. 70 (1984), p. 549.

rationally ignorant. An investor's cost of becoming informed about a charter amendment outweighs the pro rata share of benefits.

The scenario of a horde of rationally ignorant voters repeatedly misled by opportunistic managers is, however, greatly overdrawn. Institutional investors hold a majority of shares in most public corporations, and the cost of becoming informed for such sophisticated investors is quite low. First, their holdings tend to be larger than those of individuals, making an adverse information cost-benefit tradeoff questionable. Second, because governance issues typically recur across a variety of firms, information costs for diversified portfolio holders, such as institutional investors, are much smaller than posited. Third, a rationally uniformed shareholder need not assume a voting strategy of always supporting management; a mixed strategy of sometimes voting against management proposals could be costlessly adopted and produce better results in a world with managerial opportunism.[4] Indeed, not voting at all, which leaves the decision to informed voters, would seem the most rational course for the uninformed. Not voting was exactly the behavior political scientists sought to explain when they coined the term of rationally ignorant voters, which commentators on corporate law have adopted. Concern that shareholders, because of rational ignorance, will vote to impair their investment's value is, then, a questionable justification for mandatory code provisions.

Furthermore, there are effective solutions to a problem of uninformed shareholders that entail far less restrictive alternatives than mandatory substantive code provisions. Charter amendment, for example, could be subjected to supermajority voting rules. This reduces the influence of rationally ignorant voters, as the number of votes held by informed institutional investors will, with greater probability, be sufficient to block a value-decreasing proposal. Alternatively, appraisal rights, which require a firm to buy out the shares of a dissenting shareholder at a judicially determined price, could be applied to charter amendments in addition to their use in the more common setting of corporate combinations. Informed voters could

---

4. In the political science literature, where the idea of rationally ignorant voters originated, the idea was used to explain why citizens do not vote at all. A simple analysis of voting strategies of rationally ignorant shareholders is provided in Roberta Romano, "Answering the Wrong Question: The Tenuous Case for Mandatory Corporate Laws," *Columbia Law Review*, vol. 89 (1989), pp. 1599, 1607–10.

therefore recoup the loss in share value generated by approval of a value-decreasing proposal by rationally ignorant shareholders. Because a dissenting vote is required to perfect such rights, shareholders might exercise more care in voting on amendments, which would lower the probability of a harmful provision's passage.

Neither alternative scheme for policing opportunistic charter amendments, supermajority voting approval or appraisal rights, is the default rule in Delaware, although they are the defaults in some state codes. The Delaware code does not prevent firms from placing such provisions in their charters. Few, if any, Delaware corporations, however, have provisions granting appraisal rights for charter amendments. In addition, supermajority voting requirements for charter amendment, known as lockups, are most typically adopted by firms to safeguard antitakeover charter provisions. If midstream opportunism were a serious, systemic problem for investors, we would expect a different pattern: the frequency of charter provisions with expanded appraisal rights would be much higher, and the use of lockups would vary from the current practice, as promoters would have an incentive to adopt such provisions to maximize stock prices. We would also expect to find such reforms being forcefully advocated by institutional investors active in corporate governance. The absence of such activity strongly suggests that the concern of corporate law scholars about midstream opportunism is overblown.

A more important question in the mandatory-enabling debate is whether the concept of mandatory corporate law is meaningful in the first place. As noted, corporation codes are highly adaptive and functional. Rules that commentators identify as mandatory provisions have little in common with the ordinary understanding of that term, as they either can be legally side-stepped or pose a nonbinding constraint, because there is no desire by investors to deviate from them. They are laws without bite. Consider just two examples of ostensible mandatory rules that are readily avoided. One, a majority of shares must approve a merger. Management's ability to choose a transaction's form makes this rule optional. A deal can be restructured as an asset or stock acquisition and avoid a shareholder vote.[5] Two, directors must be elected by shareholders annually or through a

---

5. See, for example, Paramount Communications v. Time, Inc., 571 A.2d 1140 (Del. 1989).

classified board structure, which is viewed as a prohibition of self-perpetuating boards. There is, however, no term limit on individual directors or a mandate that shareholders control the nomination process. Nor are nonvoting or low-voting shares prohibited. Practically speaking, then, the board is self-perpetuating, as management determines its membership.

Many mandatory provisions of corporation codes are, in fact, nonbinding constraints. In several instances, the ostensible mandatory provision, such as management's duty of loyalty, would be voluntarily adopted by firms if it was not required.[6] In such situations, when there is an overwhelming consensus for the desirability of a particular rule, the claim that the provision is mandatory is not particularly meaningful. In other instances, a mandatory provision may be a housekeeping rule, with no substantive content except to impose technical clarity, such as the rule that a firm must compile the list of shareholders entitled to vote at a shareholder's meeting at least ten days before the meeting. While this particular rule will have bite in a contested election (for example, management cannot limit a challenger's access to the list by compiling it only five days before a meeting), it is difficult to divine any deep significance for corporate law from such a provision (that is, there is no significance from the use of the number ten rather than any other) or to identify a strong reason for firms to desire a number other than ten. Furthermore, such housekeeping provisions are not of principal interest to commentators concerned over the mandatory-enabling mix of corporation codes; the other form of nonbinding constraints, such as fiduciary duties, is.

More important in the history of corporation codes, when a mandatory rule's constraint becomes binding such that an increasing number of firms wish to deviate from it, the rule is repealed and revamped toward a less restrictive one. The examples of corporation codes continually progressing over the years along enabling lines are legion. For instance, voting requirements for mergers have been reduced, prohibitions on self-interested transactions have been repealed, preemptive rights and cumulative voting are no longer required, and directors' liability for breach of the duty of care can be eliminated by shareholder vote.

---

6. For elaboration of this point, see Roberta Romano, "Answering the Wrong Question," pp. 1601–2.

For a corporate law to be truly mandatory, it must be adopted by all fifty states and the District of Columbia, because firms can change their statutory domicile. The place for exploring mandatory rules in corporate law therefore involves national, not state, regulation. Restrictions or heavy taxes on reincorporation might also do the trick, but such penalties might run afoul of the commerce clause.

Federal rules are indeed mandatory and not enabling. Firms cannot opt out of the federal securities laws regulating insider trading, corporate disclosure, and takeover bids. The rationale for straying from the contractual paradigm, along with its persuasiveness, varies across contexts. Because takeover regulation has been discussed, only insider trading and disclosure regulation are considered in this chapter. The mandatory regime of state securities regulation is examined as well.

Mandatory National Laws

Given the efficacy of state competition and the contractual paradigm of corporate law, why is mandatory disclosure or insider trading regulation necessary? If disclosure of particular information benefits shareholders, why won't firms, operating as they do in competitive capital markets, voluntarily disclose the information that investors desire? Similarly, if shareholders are harmed by insider trading, is a ban as opposed to a prohibitory default rule, from which firms could opt out, truly necessary? That is, who is harmed if a firm's shareholders voluntarily opt to increase management's compensation by including trading profits? A substantial literature on these questions does not strongly support the present regulatory regime. My treatment of this topic is necessarily schematic, because it only peripherally relates to this monograph's central aim of explaining the dynamics of corporation codes. The literature, however, does cast further doubt on commentators' rose-colored view of the' efficacy of national, as opposed to state, regulation.

Mandatory Disclosure Regulation. The conventional rationale for the SEC's mandatory disclosure requirements is the argument of market failure. Information is a public good: its provision to one individual does not limit its consumption by another. My learning of a corporation's earnings, for instance, does not prevent your use of the same information. This prevents a market equilibrium that sets price equal to marginal cost, because the marginal cost to satisfy an additional user is zero. It is also often prohibitively expensive to exclude anyone from consuming (benefiting from) a public good. This creates a free-rider problem, in which the good's consumers refuse to pay their share of its production because nonpayment does not prevent their receipt of benefits. This feature also creates difficulty for market provision of the public good, because markets operate by excluding from a good's consumption individuals who are unwilling to pay the going price. Because market suppliers of a public good cannot capture the good's full value, it will be underproduced.

As is often true with a theoretical analysis, there is also a cogent counterargument that information concerning securities will be over-produced.[7] In an efficient capital market, publicly available information has no value to an investor, but new, nonpublic information is valuable: prices in efficient markets reflect all publicly available information. Thus, individuals may engage in a costly duplicative search to be the first to obtain information about a firm to beat the market—to trade on the information before it becomes public and hence to realize abnormal profits. It is not obvious whether the mandatory disclosure system discourages or encourages such waste-ful individual efforts. Even if there is a market failure, whether because of overproduction or underproduction of information, the question still remains whether producing the optimal level of infor-mation through a mandatory disclosure system is worth the cost.

Frank Easterbrook and Daniel Fischel have emphasized a varia-tion of the rationale of information as a public good to support mandatory disclosure that focuses on third-party effects (or as re-ferred to in the economics literature, externalities), settings in which firms will not have an incentive to disclose information on their own; namely, one corporation's disclosure, by revealing industrywide information, may benefit shareholders in competitor firms.[8] While the firm can charge its own investors for disclosure costs, sharehold-ers of rival firms cannot be charged for the benefits that they obtain

---

7. The classic statement of the problem is by Jack Hirshleifer, "The Private and Social Value of Information and the Reward to Inventive Activity," *American Economic Review*, vol. 61 (1971), p. 561.

8. Easterbrook and Fischel, *Economic Structure of the Corporation*, pp. 290–91.

from the information, even if they are willing to pay for it, and corporate information will thus be underproduced. Easterbrook and Fischel suggest that since some firms will have an interest in not disclosing this information, private trade associations, stock exchanges, or state competition for charters will not produce the optimal level of disclosure. Private entities cannot enforce voluntary participation in disclosure schemes,[9] and state disclosure policies will vary, because a state can profit from becoming a haven for holdouts. But this is no more than an interesting speculation. Easterbrook and Fischel offer no empirical support for their refined public-goods hypothesis. In particular, there is no evidence that third-party relevant information is the subject of the SEC's mandatory disclosure regime or that such revelations increased after adoption of the federal securities laws. Moreover, even were such data available, information on the cost-benefit trade-off of such disclosure would still be necessary to appraise the efficacy of the regime.

There has, however, been a substantial amount of empirical work investigating the more conventional rationale of public goods for mandatory disclosure. The findings tend to undercut the persuasiveness of the rationale. As George Benston has shown, firms had already been disclosing all the information that the SEC mandated on its creation except for certain sales data, and there were no significant performance differences between firms that had disclosed sales information before it was mandated and those that did not on the legislation's enactment.[10] This is a disquieting finding concerning the usefulness of a significant portion of the SEC's activities. It is also not an isolated finding that policy makers can easily ignore. The

---

9. Stock exchanges can restrict listing privileges to firms whose disclosure conforms to their requirements; before the enactment of the federal securities laws, the New York Stock Exchange had extensive disclosure requirements. Competition among exchanges could enable some firms to remain holdouts, but it is unlikely that such competition would eliminate information desired by investors because exchanges are unlikely to benefit from adopting listing conditions that do not enhance the wealth of shareholders. See, generally, Daniel R. Fischel, "Organized Exchanges and the Regulation of Dual Class Common Stock," *University of Chicago Law Review*, vol. 54 (1987), p. 119.

10. George Benston, "Required Disclosure and the Stock Market: An Evaluation of the Securities Exchange Act of 1934," *American Economic Review*, vol. 63 (1973), p. 132.

power of market forces—investor demand—to prod voluntary disclosure recurs in other contexts as well: firms with shares listed on the London Stock Exchange, for example, frequently voluntarily disclose numerous items beyond exchange requirements, presumably to lower their cost of capital.[11] In addition, several studies have investigated the impact of the federal securities laws on returns to investors in new issues, and none find evidence of substantial benefits: returns did not improve with the passage of the act.[12]

The variance of returns for new issues did decrease after enactment, but the effect of such a change on social welfare is ambiguous. If the reduced variance is the result of investors obtaining better information about the value of new issues because of the mandated disclosure, then the regulation's benefit is unquestionable. But it is equally plausible that the reduction in return variance is due to venture capitalists delaying offerings until more information about a firm's prospects can be accumulated compared with the information available when they introduced new issues before the statute's enactment.[13] Indeed, the reduced variance of returns might mean that the act caused the riskiest venture to be abandoned rather than delayed (or if not abandoned, removed from the publicly traded market of registered securities to private placements where unregistered securities can be sold).[14] If these latter scenarios better explain the empirical findings, then any gain from the reduction in variance must be offset against the cost of delaying or restricting the access of

---

11. See Gary K. Meek and S. J. Gray, "Globalization of Stock Markets and Foreign Listing Requirements: Voluntary Disclosures by Continental European Companies Listed on the London Stock Exchange," *Journal of International Business Studies*, vol. 20 (1989), p. 315.

12. For example, George J. Stigler, "Public Regulation of the Securities Market," *Journal of Business*, vol. 37 (1964), p. 117; Gregg Jarrell, "The Economic Effects of Federal Regulation of the Market for New Security Issues," *Journal of Law and Economics*, vol. 24 (1981), p. 613; Carol J. Simon, "The Effect of the 1933 Securities Act on Investor Information and the Performance of New Issues," *American Economic Review*, vol. 79 (1989), p. 295. Stigler's study was criticized by Irwin Friend and Edward S. Herman, "The SEC through a Glass Darkly," *Journal of Business*, vol. 37 (1964), p. 382, but the more recent studies of Jarrell and Simon confirm Stigler's essential results.

13. Easterbrook and Fischel, *Economic Structure of Corporate Law*, p. 313.

14. See Jarrell, "Economic Effects of Federal Regulation," p. 669.

firms to capital markets. Further evidence along these lines involves a change in accounting disclosure in 1970, when the SEC required additional line-of-business disclosure from firms with material operations in multiple industry segments (some such multisegment firms were already disclosing the information voluntarily). Studies of the change find no significant effect on stock prices, although some find a decrease in market risk.[15] This is not a finding inspiring confidence in the value-enhancing impact of SEC-mandated disclosure.

There is scant evidence on whether the benefits of the mandated disclosure regime outweigh the costs. The only study that even attempted to make a stab at this issue, which is by now somewhat dated, by Susan Phillips and Richard Zecher, conservatively estimated direct costs for 1975 at $406 million, with a projection of $1 billion for 1980, but it had no handle on quantifying benefits.[16] In 1975, firms spent ten times more than this estimate on voluntary disclosures. Phillips and Zecher's estimate is conservative because it excludes the SEC's cost of administering the system and any allocation of firms' overhead expenses in preparing documents or establishing accounting or auditing systems to meet mandated disclosure standards. The cost of the mandatory disclosure regime, then, appears substantial; whether firms pass through the full costs of the regime to investors is unknown. Moreover, if regulation is producing any benefit, it is likely to be quite small in relation to what firms voluntarily provide.

The per capita cost of mandatory disclosure appears small, and the bearers of the cost—corporate owners and consumers—are not an organized political interest group. If we consider who is likely to benefit from the regulation, two well-organized groups can be identified as clear winners: (1) financial analysts and other market professionals who obtain corporate information free and (2) accountants,

---

15. For example, Bertrand Horwitz and Richard Kolodny, "Line of Business Reporting: An Analysis of an SEC Disclosure Rule," *Bell Journal of Economics*, vol. 8 (1977), p. 234; Richard R. Simonds and Daniel W. Collins, "Line of Business Reporting and Security Prices: An Analysis of an SEC Disclosure Rule: Comment," *Bell Journal of Economics*, vol. 9 (1978), p. 646; Bertrand Horwitz and Richard Kolodny, "Line of Business Reporting: A Rejoinder," *Bell Journal of Economics*, vol. 9 (1978), p. 659.

16. Susan Phillips and Richard Zecher, *The SEC and the Public Interest* (Cambridge: MIT Press, 1981), p. 51.

attorneys, and other professionals who produce the required documents.[17] The regulatory regime subsidizes the former's search effort, and its administration is an employment act for the latter. Furthermore, as noted, it is problematic whether shareholders obtain any benefit from the regulation. This analysis suggests that the interests of those paying for the regulatory system may not be adequately factored into the political process compared with those of the regulation's beneficiaries. It also suggests exercising caution in assuming that the output of the federal securities regulatory process is purely public-spirited, notwithstanding its legislative origins as a reaction to trading scandals, the 1929 stock market crash, and the depression.

There is a potentially important mechanism that could counterbalance the interests and activities of those who benefit from the SEC's mandatory disclosure: competition from foreign markets. As international capital markets become increasingly integrated, costly and inefficient regulatory regimes encounter competition from markets whose regimes investors and issuers prefer. If investors do not value (that is, do not wish to pay for) the higher U.S. level of required corporate disclosure compared with that of other nations, they will invest in firms listed on foreign exchanges, and U.S. exchange listings will decline. The U.S. share of the world capital market has already begun to shrink, although the full force of international competition has yet to be felt, because the trend to a global market is quite recent.[18] The market capitalization of U.S. securities markets, for example, was 39 percent of the world total in 1989, compared with 66⅔ percent in 1970.[19] In addition, during the 1980s, foreign purchases and sales of U.S. stocks increased fivefold, while U.S. purchases and sales of foreign stocks increased ninefold.[20] Finally, by 1988, nearly 7 percent of world equity market

---

17. Ibid.

18. See David E. Van Zandt, "The Regulatory and Institutional Conditions for an International Securities Market," *Virginia Journal of International Law*, vol. 32 (1991), p. 47.

19. Frederick D. S. Choi and Richard M. Levich, "International Accounting Diversity: Does It Impact Market Participants?" National Bureau of Economic Research Working Paper 3590 (Cambridge, Mass. 1991), p. 1.

20. Ibid.

capitalization was held by cross-border investors.[21]

The Eurobond market, an international market consisting of an informal network of international market makers and dealers trading bonds issued by international bank syndicates, provides a good example of the impact on regulators of international market competition. Some sense of the size of this market is provided by table 5–1, which shows that the amount of newly issued Eurobonds has been increasing substantially, from $81 billion (U.S.) in 1984 to $276 billion (U.S.) in 1992. The Eurobond market is self-regulated: because Eurobonds are sold exclusively in countries other than the country in whose currency the securities are denominated, they are subject to no government's regulation. This market developed as a response to domestic market regulation: foreign issuers, for example, can sell bonds to U.S. investors in the Eurobond market while avoiding the SEC's disclosure requirements.[22] Recent regulatory changes by the SEC relaxing disclosure requirements for certain private placements under rule 144A in 1990, and for certain public offerings under the shelf registration rule 415 in the 1980s, are viewed by commentators in international finance as efforts, at least in part, to improve the competitiveness of the U.S. domestic bond market in relation to the Eurobond market.[23]

The trend to globalization of the capital market has created pressure on the SEC to ease its disclosure requirements for foreign issuers wishing to sell securities in U.S. markets.[24] A particular sticking point is the SEC's requirement that foreign firms reconcile

---

21. Frederick D. S. Choi and Richard M. Levich, *The Capital Market Effects of International Accounting Diversity* (Homewood, Ill.: Dow Jones-Irwin, 1990), p. 12.

22. David K. Eiteman, Arthur I. Stonehill, and Michael H. Moffett, *Multinational Business Finance*, 6th ed. (Reading, Mass.: Addison-Wesley, 1992), pp. 327–28; Alan C. Shapiro, *Multinational Financial Management*, 4th ed. (Boston: Allyn and Bacon, 1992), pp. 588–89; Choi and Levich, *Capital Market Effects of International Accounting Diversity*, pp. 33, 58. Investors and issuers also avoid domestic tax and monetary regulation by using the Eurobond market. For a description of this market, see the above sources and Bruno Solnik, *International Investments*, 2d ed. (Reading, Mass.: Addison-Wesley, 1991), pp. 172–75.

23. Eiteman, Stonehill, and Moffett, *Multinational Business Finance*, pp. 328–29; Shapiro, *Multinational Financial Management*, p. 590.

24. See, for example, Franklin R. Edwards, "Listing of Foreign Securities on U.S. Exchanges," *Journal of Applied Corporate Finance*, vol. 5 (Winter 1993), p. 28.

TABLE 5–1
EUROBOND ISSUES BY CURRENCY, 1984–1992
(in billions of U.S. dollars)

Currency	1984	1985	1986	1987	1988	1989	1990	1991	1992
U.S. dollar	65.3	96.8	118.1	58.1	74.5	117.5	70.0	76.9	103.2
Deutsche mark	4.3	9.6	17.1	15.0	23.7	16.4	18.3	19.9	33.8
Yen	1.2	6.6	18.5	22.6	15.9	15.6	22.8	35.7	33.7
Sterling	4.0	6.1	10.6	15.0	23.6	18.5	20.9	25.7	23.3
French franc	—	1.1	3.5	1.8	2.3	4.5	9.4	17.0	24.3
ECU[a]	2.9	6.9	7.1	7.4	11.2	12.6	17.9	31.6	21.3
Canadian dollar	2.1	2.9	5.1	6.0	13.1	12.5	6.4	22.5	15.6
Other	1.6	6.6	7.7	14.6	14.5	15.2	14.4	19.2	20.9
Total	81.4	136.6	187.7	140.5	178.8	212.8	180.1	248.5	276.1

a. European currency unit.
SOURCE: Organization for Economic Coordination and Development, *Financial Market Trends* (Paris: OECD, 1989, 1993).

their financial statements to U.S. accounting principles (referred to as U.S. GAAP, generally accepted accounting principles). Because such restatement is expensive, this requirement deters foreign listings on U.S. exchanges, weakening their competitive position compared with foreign markets, particularly the London Stock Exchange.[25] The regulation is also largely ineffective: the SEC's stricter listing requirements that prevent foreign issuers from listing their securities on U.S. exchanges do not, in fact, prevent U.S. investors from purchasing such securities. Rather, they are forced to purchase them in foreign markets instead, which increases their costs—foreign markets are often subject to transaction taxes and have higher commission fees, while offering less liquidity than U.S. markets.

There is little evidence that U.S. investors would be harmed if the SEC followed a practice of reciprocity, rather than reconciliation, for foreign securities. Foreign nations' stock markets are as efficient—information is incorporated into stock prices as quickly—as U.S. markets, despite differing reporting requirements for issuers.[26] In addition, empirical studies suggest that foreign firms' restatements under U.S. GAAP are not informative, for firms' restatements are not accompanied by significant positive stock price effects.[27] Finally, compliance with U.S. GAAP requirements by foreign firms is not always informative for investors: GAAP requirements are, for example, tailored to tax laws, and restatement of foreign financial statements into U.S. GAAP is therefore often misleading for firms subject to disparate tax regimes.[28]

The SEC has eased its reconciliation requirement for some firms, and this trend will continue, given investors' demand for

---

25. See William J. Baumol and Burton G. Malkiel, "Redundant Regulation of Foreign Security Trading and U.S. Competitiveness," *Journal of Applied Corporate Finance*, vol. 5 (Winter 1993), pp. 19, 20–21.

26. See Edwards, "Listing of Foreign Securities"; Baumol and Malkiel, "Redundant Regulation of Foreign Security Trading and U.S. Competitiveness."

27. Both Edwards, "Listing of Foreign Securities," and Baumol and Malkiel, "Redundant Regulation of Foreign Security Trading and U.S. Competitiveness," review these studies.

28. Baumol and Malkiel, "Redundant Regulation of Foreign Security Trading and U.S. Competitiveness," p. 20.

international holdings to diversify their portfolios and U.S. exchanges' concern over losing trading business to foreign competitors.[29] A fair prediction of future trends is that as the capital market
becomes increasingly globalized, the SEC's domestic firm disclosure
policy will have to be reconfigured to the extent that the cost-benefit
calculus for such regulation is unfavorable for investors, as it appears.

There is, however, a potentially dangerous impediment to the
international competitive pressure on regulators of national capital
markets: interjurisdictional harmonization. Several institutions are
engaged in efforts at harmonizing capital market regulation: the
International Organization of Securities Commissioners, International Accounting Standards Commission and, for members of the
European Economic Community, directives issued by the EC. These
efforts have to date not been successful. The EC's accounting
directives, for instance, permit significant variation, because EC
members could not agree on abolishing what are perceived to be
critical national differences.[30] And the IASC has no authority to
implement its proposals.[31] If harmonization efforts are influenced by
noninvestor interests, as occurs in the corporate law harmonization
in the European Community discussed in chapter 6, they will not
only undercut the pressure of competition to prod market regulators
to adopt more cost-effective disclosure requirements but could also
result in regulations whose cost-benefit calculus works for noninvestor interests. Because the use of accounts differs across coun-

---

29. In 1991, the SEC reached a special agreement with Canada providing for
listing reciprocity of seasoned issuers; "Multijurisdictional Disclosure and Modifi-
cation to the Current Registration and Reporting System for Canadian Issuers,"
Securities Act Release 6902, Exchange Act Release 29354 [1991 Transfer Binder],
Federal Securities Law Reporter (Commercial Clearing House), paragraph 84,812
(June 21, 1991). In addition, the SEC has modified its requirements for certain
foreign private issuers under form 20-F to permit discussion of material differences,
rather than actual reconciliation of foreign firm's statements and U.S. GAAP. It also
loosened disclosure requirements for certain domestic private and public placements, as noted.

30. See, for example, Paul Rutteman, "International Pressures for the Harmonisation of Accounting," in A. Hopwood, ed., *International Pressures for Accounting
Change* (Hemel Hempstead, Hertfordshire, U.K.: Prentice Hall International,
1989), pp. 57, 58–59.

31. Ibid., pp. 67–68.

tries—they are used in the United Kingdom to indicate performance, and hence are addressed to investors, whereas in Germany they are linked to the distributability of profits and tax requirements, and are thereby written for tax collectors, unions, and creditors[32]—there is a real possibility that any regulatory output of interjurisdictional harmonization will not benefit investors.

Insider Trading Regulation. Objections to the federal prohibition on insider trading are twofold: (1) insider trading improves market efficiency, as the trades carry information that move prices in the right direction (presumably at a time when it would be against the corporation's interest to disclose the information directly); and (2) insider trading profits are an effective form of executive compensation that encourages managerial risk taking.[33]

While many rationales have been offered for the prohibition, including fairness across investors, ensuring equal access to information by all market participants, and enhancing market efficiency by forcing insiders to disclose important corporate information before they can trade, the most persuasive one extends the traditional law of fiduciary duty: corporate information belongs to shareholders and, as with other business property, cannot be used by managers to favor themselves at shareholders' expense.[34] The fiduciary justification does not, however, address the underlying issue of whether a trading ban should be the province of the national government as opposed to the states and, more important, whether it should be mandatory. For as Dennis Carlton and Daniel Fischel and Jonathan Macey contend, the business property rationale is related to the contractual view of the corporation, as the allocation of the property right in information is subject to the parties' contracts. This perspective permits firms to tailor statutory defaults to their particular circumstances, such as opting out of an insider trading prohibition, if shareholders so desire.[35]

---

32. Ibid., p. 58.

33. See Henry Manne's iconoclastic *Insider Trading and the Stock Market* (New York: Free Press, 1966), which was not taken seriously until the 1980s, and Dennis Carlton and Daniel Fischel, "The Regulation of Insider Trading," *Stanford Law Review*, vol. 35 (1983), p. 857.

34. For a cogent review of the rationales, see Jonathan R. Macey, *Insider Trading* (Washington, D.C.: AEI Press, 1991).

35. Carlton and Fischel, "Regulation of Insider Trading"; Macey, *Insider Trading*.

One of the more interesting rationales supporting the insider trading ban involves enforcement difficulties. The economic analysis of criminal law indicates that optimal deterrence involves a trade-off between detection and punishment—the lower the probability of being caught, the higher must the penalty be to deter criminal conduct, since the lawbreaker compares the benefits and costs of criminal activity.[36] Frank Easterbrook suggests that because detection of insider trading is difficult, the penalty necessary to deter managers from trading may be so high that it cannot be imposed by a private corporation; this would necessitate public enforcement, which can impose criminal punishment if substantial financial penalties would simply render a defendant insolvent.[37] Furthermore, if firms cannot privately enforce an insider trading prohibition, then managers who intend to trade on inside information can include a ban in their charter with impunity. Investors will not be outsmarted: they will pay less for common stock because honest managers cannot be distinguished from the dishonest. Honest managers thus suffer from the decreased value at which they can sell shares in their firms. Public enforcement of a ban eliminates this welfare loss by raising penalties sufficiently to deter cheating by dishonest managers. There is, however, a practical weakness with this explanation. Until the 1980s, cases seeking criminal penalties for insider trading, rather than civil sanctions, were unheard of.

In his work with Daniel Fischel, Easterbrook acknowledges that the benefits from public enforcement of an insider trading ban do not clearly justify mandatory participation in a ban.[38] Fischel and Easterbrook offer one further possible justification, that public enforcement may not be effective unless all firms ban insider trading. But they do not indicate why enforcement would fail if only a subset of the corporate population adopts an insider trading prohibition. I cannot come up with any reason for such a scenario.[39] If the insider

---

36. See Gary S. Becker, "Crime and Punishment: An Economic Approach," *Journal of Political Economy*, vol. 76 (1968), p. 169.

37. See Frank Easterbrook, "Insider Trading as an Agency Problem," in J. Pratt and R. Zeckhauser, eds., *Principals and Agents: The Structure of Business* (Boston: Harvard Business School Press, 1985), p. 81.

38. Easterbrook and Fischel, *Economic Structure of Corporate Law*, p. 264.

39. Macey also emphasizes this point in *Insider Trading*, pp. 40–41.

trading ban is not mandatory, then there is a more pragmatic question: why should we permit the public resources of the criminal justice system to be used for these particular private purposes (that is, to enforce private contract provisions banning insider trading)? We could, however, charge firms for such enforcement services, through payment of additional fees on registration of their securities.

A final problem with the enforcement explanation is the question whether the difficulty of enforcing an insider trading prohibition is significantly lessened when shifted to the public sector. An empirical study by Michael Dooley of insider trading regulation during the 1970s concludes that public enforcement was ineffective.[40] The situation could be different in recent years, however, because penalties for insider trading have been substantially increased, as have criminal prosecutions.[41] H. Nejat Seyhun examined whether the statutory increase in sanctions in 1984 deterred insider trading.[42] He found that, to the contrary, insider trading, and the profitability of such trades, significantly increased after the sanctions were raised. But there is also evidence of a deterrent effect for certain kinds of inside information: insider purchases before takeover announcements significantly decreased after the sanction reform.[43] Because insider trading sanctions were increased again in 1988, which is beyond the period covered by Seyhun's study, a more definitive evaluation of the enforcement rationale for an insider trading ban must await further research.

Although no study has even attempted the daunting task of estimating the cost of administering the insider trading ban, empirical research on insider trading has resolved some questions. We do know that market efficiency is enhanced by insider trades: on days

---

40. Michael Dooley, "Enforcement of Insider Trading Restrictions," *Virginia Law Review*, vol. 66 (1980), p. 1.

41. Insider Trading Sanctions Act of 1984, Public Law No. 98-376, 98 Stat. 1264; Insider Trading and Securities Fraud Enforcement Act of 1988, Public Law No. 100-704, 102 Stat. 4677 (adding new §§ 20A and 21A to the 1934 act).

42. H. Nejat Seyhun, "The Effectiveness of the Insider-Trading Sanctions," *Journal of Law and Economics*, vol. 35 (1992), p. 149.

43. For inexplicable reasons, Seyhun states that this decline is a reaction to court cases on insider trading rather than the sanctions legislation. But his data do not support such a contention, as pretakeover trades significantly decrease after the legislation as well as after the court cases.

that insiders trade, prices move significantly in the same direction as when the information is finally disclosed.[44] These data can be viewed as supporting opponents of the ban, who emphasize the ban's adverse effect on market efficiency. Proponents of the ban, however, could also view the data as evidence of the validity of their concerns over equal access and ownership of corporate property, since if there was no price movement on the insiders' trades, there could not be any redistribution from outsiders to insiders from such trading. In line with these concerns, there is also evidence that trading by insiders is quite profitable: several studies found that an investor following the strategy of copying insiders' trades would have made abnormal trading profits, although some studies conclude that the insiders' trades are not related to imminent information releases.[45]

Given the limited empirical evidence supporting or opposing insider trading regulation, it may be useful to ask who benefits from the legislation. Determining which shareholders gain or lose from insider trading regulation is tricky, but doing so is important from the perspective of those who advocate insider trading restrictions on grounds of fairness. Investors following a strategy of buy and hold may be less likely to be adversely affected by insider trading than active traders, for they are not engaged in timing strategies, for which information releases matter. But as Hersh Shefrin and Meir Statman note, if (all) investors naively believe that the prohibition on insider trading is effective, when as the empirical studies suggest it is not, then even passive investors could be losers, for they would not factor in a trading disadvantage when originally purchasing shares and therefore would overpay.[46] While the usual policy approach to situa-

---

44. See, for example, Lisa K. Muelbroek, "An Empirical Analysis of Illegal Insider Trading," *Journal of Finance*, vol. 47 (1992), p. 1661.

45. See Jeffrey F. Jaffe, "Special Information and Insider Trading," *Journal of Business*, vol. 47 (1974), p. 410; J. E. Finnerty, "Insiders and Market Efficiency," *Journal of Finance*, vol. 31 (1976), p. 1141; H. Nejat Seyhun, "Insiders' Profits, Costs of Trading and Market Efficiency," *Journal of Financial Economics*, vol. 16 (1986), p. 189; J. Elliott, D. Morse, and G. Richardson, "The Association between Insider Trading and Information Announcements," *RAND Journal of Economics*, vol. 15 (1984), p. 521; D. Givoly and D. Palmon, "Insider Trading and the Exploitation of Inside Information: Some Empirical Evidence," *Journal of Business*, vol. 58 (1985), p. 69.

46. Hersh Shefrin and Meir Statman, *Ethics, Fairness, Efficiency, and Financial*

tions in which individuals make serious cognitive errors is paternalistic, the policy implication in the insider trading setting is the opposite: Shefrin and Statman suggest that making insider trading legal would benefit such investors, because they would no longer be misled into complacency but would be forewarned of insiders' trading advantage and would adjust their purchase prices accordingly.[47]

Henry Manne also contends that passive investors are not harmed by insider trading.[48] Manne makes this point while criticizing a new argument by economists that supports insider trading regulation: because insiders are indistinguishable from other traders in the anonymous trading of modern capital markets, market makers risk purchasing (selling) shares at too high (low) a price and accordingly charge a higher fee for their market-making services than they would if insiders could not trade by increasing the bid-ask spread, the difference between a stock's offer and ask prices, to cover their losses.[49] Because all investors bear this trading cost, the argument goes, they would benefit from an insider trading ban. Manne contends that the cost is borne primarily by investors who trade frequently, since those who buy and hold will over time earn the average return to both insiders and outsiders, which includes gains from inside information released after their stock purchases.[50] The implication

---

Markets (Charlottesville, Va.: Research Foundation of the Institute of Chartered Financial Analysts, 1992), p. 84.

47. Ibid. As a doctrinal matter, the Supreme Court eliminated fairness justifications for the insider trading prohibition when it held in *Chiarella* that a breach of fiduciary duty was a prerequisite for violating the insider trading ban of SEC rule 10b-5, rather than unequal access to information. See Chiarella v. United States 445 U.S. 222 (1980).

48. Henry G. Manne, "Insider Trading: Risk Premiums and Confidence Games," George Mason University School of Law, Law and Economics Working Paper 93-001 (Fairfax, Va., 1993).

49. See, for example, H. Nejat Seyhun, "Insiders' Profits, Costs of Trading, and Market Efficiency," *Journal of Financial Economics*, vol. 16 (1986), p. 189.

50. Manne, "Insider Trading: Risk Premiums and Confidence Games," p. 7. Manne further contends that if insiders can also make markets, they will offer better prices (higher offer and lower ask prices) than noninsider market makers. Either such competition will eliminate the "insider trading tax" of higher bid-ask spreads, or insiders will charge a premium somewhat below that of other market makers, income that the market will treat as a substitute for other forms of compensation;

of this distribution of the cost of insider trading is a lifting of the ban, because frequent traders are most likely gamblers or speculators, whose activities, he suggests, are not worthy of federal protection.

There is one class of identifiable winners from an insider trading ban. As Jonathan Macey notes, informational advantages are inevitable in a securities market; when corporate insiders are stripped of their edge, the advantage goes to the group next in line, market professionals.[51] Macey further maintains that this outcome is the worst possible for shareholders. His contention is that if managers can trade on inside information, the firm and hence shareholders receive some benefit—managers' salaries should be reduced by the expected profits of insider trading. No such benefit accrues to shareholders, when the trading profits from information go to market professionals. Thus, his analysis, as with that of Shefrin and Statman, undermines a shareholder protection–based rationale for insider trading regulation. There is, at least, a means of testing Macey's thesis: in many countries, insider trading has only recently been prohibited. Managerial compensation could be compared before and after the legislative change to see if the hypothesized tradeoff occurs, and stock prices of securities firms could be examined. If the market shares Macey's assessment of who gains from the ban, these firms should experience positive abnormal returns on the announcement of the legislation.

As with mandatory disclosure, while elegant theoretical analyses can be marshaled for prohibiting insider trading, empirical confirmation that it benefits shareholders is thin, and support for mandating a prohibition is even more problematic. In evaluating what we know about the efficacy of the mandatory disclosure regime, Easterbrook and Fischel have it right when they conclude that the arguments in its favor are, at best, inconclusive.[52] The same assessment is appro-

---

under either scenario outside investors do not bear any cost from insider trading; ibid., p. 18.

51. Macey, *Insider Trading*, pp. 14–18. He contends that after the Supreme Court held that a fiduciary duty was a prerequisite for insider trading in Chiarella v. United States, 445 U.S. 222 (1980), immunizing market professionals from liability, market professionals successfully lobbied for vigorous enforcement of the insider trading rules to eliminate their competition for information.

52. Easterbrook and Fischel, *Economic Structure of Corporate Law*, p. 314.

priate for the mandatory ban on insider trading. A more sensible public policy would be to make the federal securities laws optional, applicable to firms at the shareholders' choice. Given concerns over management's advantage in using the proxy mechanism and the managerial conflict of interest involved in the proposal, unlike takeover statutes, the default should be set at prohibition, with firms having to opt out of the insider trading regime. I would predict little substantive change from this recommendation, as I expect that shareholders will want uniformly to retain an insider trading ban. But there is no convincing reason to remove this issue from shareholder consideration. In Germany, for example, where limits on insider trading have been optional, 90 percent of the publicly traded securities are issued by corporations that have opted into the regulation.[53]

If the policy toward disclosure and insider trading were enabling, then there would be no compelling reason to retain national jurisdiction over securities regulation. If regulatory authority were returned to the states, however, jurisdiction over securities transactions would have to be changed from the current transactional basis to the corporate law conflicts rule of statutory domicile. Otherwise, firms with shareholders residing in different states could be subject to diverse default rules, and opting out of multiple regimes, which could vary over time as the firm's shareholders changed, would be exceedingly complex. In fact, it is probably more sensible to retain federal jurisdiction while experimenting with an enabling framework. Retaining federal jurisdiction also allows experimenting with an alternative to the firm-based option suggested here, an exchange-based regulatory scheme. The national exchanges might be quite effective at designing optimal regulations of insider trading in their listing requirements, as they have an interest in maximizing trading, which should be related to the extent of insider activity. But a more important lesson can be drawn from the discussion: the experience under the federal securities laws suggests that the widely shared, yet rarely articulated, belief that a national corporation law, whether

---

53. Bernhard Bergman, *Inside Information and Securities Trading* (London: Graham & Trotman, 1991), p. 80. Bergman contends that the reason for the high acceptance of trading restrictions is that there are no sanctions for violations, but he does not provide evidence in support of this contention. The 10 percent not covered are small companies with controlling shareholders, whose stock trades in a very limited market.

mandatory or enabling, will better serve shareholders than state chartering is mistaken.

State Securities Regulation

The federal securities laws expressly preserve the states' power to regulate securities transactions. States have exercised this power under securities regimes that are separate from corporation codes and, like the federal statutes, are mandatory. The regulations, known as blue sky laws, consist of antifraud provisions and registration requirements for securities and the brokers and dealers selling them. The first blue sky law was enacted in Kansas in 1911, with a stated goal of preventing fraudulent securities sales (by operators who would sell shares in the blue sky) and, as Jonathan Macey and Geoffrey Miller note, with an indirect benefit for the regulation's lobbyists, local bankers, who were losing deposits to securities sales, and for farmers and small businesses, who relied on bank financing (and would have improved access to credit on eliminating out-of-state competitors).[54] While all states have some type of blue sky law, there is tremendous variety across regimes. The most significant distinction is between states that have followed Kansas's lead, with an approach to regulation, termed merit regulation, quite distinctive from the federal disclosure approach and the others. In a state with merit regulation, registration is conditioned on the securities' meeting a standard of investment worthiness or merit.[55]

The determination of an issue's merit is left to a state official's discretion. While the merit review standard varies across states, common criteria include offering price (typically the price must be no more than a particular multiple of earnings), underwriter fees, insider compensation, and voting rights. Some critics of merit regulation emphasize both the adverse effect on capital formation of the

---

54. See Jonathan R. Macey and Geoffrey P. Miller, "Origin of the Blue Sky Laws," *Texas Law Review*, vol. 70 (1991), p. 347.

55. A majority of states have merit language in their securities statutes, but less than a dozen are considered tough merit states, that is, states that "frequently and systematically raise objections on merit grounds" to securities offerings; Ad Hoc Subcommittee on Merit Regulation of the State Regulation of Securities Committee of the American Bar Association, "Report on State Merit Regulation of Securities Offerings," *Business Lawyer*, vol. 41 (1986), pp. 785, 790.

offering price criterion and the typical exemptions for shares in companies already trading on national exchanges: by conditioning approval on a price-earnings ratio or prior listing, the regulation discriminates against new companies in favor of more established companies and hence inhibits the ability of new firms to raise capital.[56]

Other commentators, reviewing the criteria involving corporate governance requirements, suggest that blue sky laws are illegitimate efforts at regulating corporate governance by the back door—by a securities commissioner rather than a corporation code.[57] A commissioner may disagree not only with the legislature's enabling code but also with another state's code and exercise an extraterritorial reach on corporate governance (that is, if the state of incorporation of the firm seeking to register securities permits variation from a mandatory provision in the registering state's code, the commissioner can override the incorporation state by imposing compliance with his state's code as a registration condition). Given that by merit review a state could blunt the organizational choice produced by state competition, an interesting finding is that the states most active in the corporate chartering market were slow to enact blue sky legislation.[58] But the effect on state competition of merit review is not as significant as initially appears because firms can avoid the regulation by not offering securities in states with burdensome registration requirements. Extraterritorial efforts at regulating corporate governance through securities regulation are successful only when undertaken by a large state, such as California, whose investor population is too substantial for promoters to ignore. Even then, market demand can limit the regulations' effectiveness: there are several instances involving mutual fund shares, where residents who wished to invest in the funds successfully pressured state officials to register the shares by waiving blue sky restrictions on mutual fund holdings and fees.[59]

---

56. See Marianne M. Jennings, Bruce K. Childers, and Ronald J. Kudla, "Federalism to an Advantage: The Demise of State Blue Sky Laws under the Uniform Securities Act," *Akron Law Review*, vol. 19 (1986), pp. 395, 399–400.

57. See Harold S. Bloomenthal, "Blue Sky Regulation and the Theory of Overkill," *Wayne Law Review*, vol. 15 (1969), p. 1447.

58. See Macey and Miller, "Origin of the Blue Sky Laws," p. 378.

59. Kevin G. Salwen, "State Laws Are Often Overkill, Some Say," *Wall Street Journal*, July 20, 1987, p. 35.

Merit regulation has more in common with consumer protection statutes than with corporation codes. It assumes a paternalistic attitude toward investors, seeking to shield them from investments that regulators deem excessively risky or expensive. In contrast to the federal disclosure approach, merit regulation is skeptical of even informed investor choices; it permits regulators to remove investments from the market rather than let the market, armed with full disclosure of material information, determine whether an investment is worth the risk. The efficacy of merit regulation has been continuously debated in the literature. It entails the tradeoff of any additional benefit accruing to investors in stemming promoter fraud from merit instead of disclosure regulation against the increased cost of capital to new firms and consequent opportunity losses from businesses that cannot finance operations. Although there have been no studies of the cost of merit regulation or the effectiveness of merit regulation in preventing fraud, several studies have sought to evaluate the benefit of merit review by comparing the performance of securities registered in a merit state with that of securities either denied registration or withdrawn from the state and sold in another (nonmerit) state. An offering may be withdrawn for numerous reasons, including anticipation of denial because state officials expressed concern with the application as well as nonmerit review reasons, such as poor market conditions, failure to qualify under federal securities laws, or a filing in error when an exemption was available.

A common finding across studies is that the return to securities in nonmerit states is higher than the return in merit states in the short term (measured variously as one day, one month, or one year, depending on the study), and returns decline more over the long term.[60] Where the risk of the two sets of securities is measured, securities in the nonmerit state are riskier. These findings are not surprising: regulators succeed in what they set out to do, eliminating

---

60. The studies are reviewed in the most recent study, commissioned by the Business Law Section of the American Bar Association, by David J. Brophy and Joseph A. Verga, "The Influence of Merit Regulation on the Return Performance of Initial Public Offerings," University of Michigan School of Business Administration Working Paper 91-19 (Ann Arbor, 1991). Only one study that they review found no significant difference in the returns of merit and nonmerit state securities; Gary D. Levine, "A Challenge to Massachusetts Merit Regulation of Securities: An Empirical Analysis," *Boston Bar Journal* (January–February 1982).

riskier securities from their state's new issue market. But they do not demonstrate that such a policy is desirable. To conclude so, additional evidence is necessary, such as finding that investors in merit states are more risk averse than those in nonmerit states,[61] to explain why such securities should not be offered in a particular state, as well as a finding that state officials can evaluate firms' disclosure information better than investors can for assessing securities' risk. If promoter fraud, not investment risk, is the regulatory concern, then the requisite evidence involves the cause of the subsequent price decline of nonapproved issues, that is, a demonstration that it is related to fraudulent sales practices rather than to investment risk.

Given the limited evidence of benefit from merit regulation, the view of investors as sophisticated consumers of financial information emphasized in this monograph, as well as by corporation codes, indicates that disclosure, and not merit regulation, is the most sensible policy approach for securities regulation. This wisdom is reflected in the market itself, for several important commercial states, such as New York, have never adopted merit regulation and others, such as Illinois and Michigan, have repealed or severely restricted merit review in the past decade.[62] State securities regulation is, in fact, an area where the benefits of federalism again demonstrate the usefulness of competition. There is substantial experimentation across the states in securities regulation, evident not only in the historical diversity of regulatory arrangements and evolution within state securities codes but also in enforcement practice: only a few states actively engage in merit review.[63]

The coverage of merit regulation is, moreover, quite limited in

---

61. Merit regulation is not necessarily warranted even if the state's investors are extremely risk averse, because they can combine investments in risky new issues with those in riskless securities like Treasury bills and achieve an equivalent risk-return package to a portfolio consisting of only state-approved new issues.

62. For a discussion of these developments, see Mark A. Sargent, "Blue Sky Law: The Challenge to Merit Regulation—Part 1," *Securities Regulation Law Journal*, vol. 12 (1985), p. 276.

63. Of the states with merit statutory language, no more than a dozen appear to enforce merit standards rigorously at any one time, the particular states changing with changes in securities commissioners. Hugh H. Makens, "Who Speaks for the Investor? An Evaluation of the Assault on Merit Regulation," *University of Baltimore Law Review*, vol. 13 (1984), p. 435.

practice. Most states exempt securities listed on a national exchange or in specified industry manuals (such as Moody's) from their registration requirements, as well as privately placed securities that meet SEC tests for private placement registration. Secondary trading of securities is also typically exempted. In fact, the principal method by which states have restricted merit review is by increasing exemptions from review rather than by constraining officials' discretion. Besides these numerous exemptions, a state's merit review can be avoided by the firm's not offering securities to investors in that state. Individuals who wish to invest in such firms are not shut out of the market: typically, they can buy the securities in unsolicited secondary market transactions. The timing of investment is restricted, however, as they cannot participate in the initial public offering, and the largest gains from such purchases accrue to the original investors, as they are obtained on the first day of trading.[64]

The important fact from the viewpoint of federalism is that the effect of merit regulation on corporate equity capital has become increasingly contained over time, and it is primarily a nuisance, as the dynamic of state competition, however slowly, prods states to discard cumbersome arrangements with dubious benefits. Given this trend, there is little reason to seek preemption, particularly if it could result in establishing national merit review.[65] The experience with national securities regulation is sufficiently problematic to raise doubts about its emulation in other spheres.

Federal Criminalization of State Fiduciary Duty

The federal securities laws are mandatory supplements to state corporation codes and, partly by default, have largely replaced state control. The extensive disclosure requirements of the SEC, for example, may eviscerate state efforts in such regulation, as the states tend to piggyback on its framework and exempt established firms complying with SEC registration requirements from merit regulation, a strategy that is also least burdensome for large corporations.

---

64. Brophy and Verga, "Influence of Merit Regulation on Return Performance," pp. 8, 20–22, 85.

65. See Roberta S. Karmel, "Blue-Sky Merit Regulation: Benefit to Investors or Burden on Commerce?" *Brooklyn Law Review*, vol. 53 (1987), p. 105.

Similarly, the expansive development of federal regulation of insider trading led investor-plaintiffs to abandon state claims for the federal courts. Only in the takeover area have the states vigorously sought to complement the federal regime. In recent years, there has been a movement by federal prosecutors to criminalize fiduciary duties under the federal mail and wire fraud statutes. This has an impact similar to the securities laws, in its replacement of state corporate law. In a series of federal cases, managers have been held criminally liable for conduct that would not have provided the basis for civil liability in a shareholder suit because the action, at worst, breached the duty of care, not self-dealing, and few courts have ever found such conduct wrongful.[66] In a review of cases concerning directors' and officers' liability to shareholders, Joseph Bishop concluded that finding a suit holding a director liable for a breach of duty based on negligence as opposed to self-dealing was like searching for "very few needles in a very large haystack."[67]

Federal mail and wire fraud statutes make it a crime to use the mail or electronic transmissions to execute a scheme or artifice to defraud for the purpose of obtaining money or property by false representations.[68] In using such broad statutes for jurisdiction to prosecute corporate officers for conduct implicating only the duty of care rather than self-dealing, prosecutors were permitted to contend that the requisite scheme to defraud is the deprivation of the shareholders' intangible right to receive honest services (that is, violation of a fiduciary duty to act honestly is a scheme to defraud). This prosecutorial bootstrapping is an extension of the reasoning in cases prosecuting public officials involved in kickback schemes for

---

66. For identification of this trend and a detailed discussion of the cases, see John C. Coffee, "Does 'Unlawful' Mean 'Criminal'? Reflections on the Disappearing Tort/ Crime Distinction in American Law," *Boston University Law Review*, vol. 71 (1991), p. 193. A parallel development is the use of the Racketeer Influenced Corrupt Organizations Act in both criminal and civil cases; the underlying pattern of criminal activity that is required by RICO is, in such instances, a mail or wire fraud, based on activity that is itself not criminal, such as a fiduciary breach.

67. Joseph W. Bishop, "Sitting Ducks and Decoy Ducks: New Trends in the Indemnification of Corporate Directors and Officers," *Yale Law Journal*, vol. 77 (1968), pp. 1078, 1099.

68. Federal jurisdiction is derived from the use of mechanisms of interstate commerce (mail or wire).

defrauding citizens of the intangible right of the officials' duty to provide honest and faithful services.[69]

A good example of the problems with this type of prosecution is *United States v. Siegel.*[70] A corporate officer who created an off-book account (using unrecorded cash sales) to facilitate questionable payments to buyers and labor unions was convicted of wire fraud, even though he did not misappropriate any funds and acted to benefit the corporation. The amounts in question averaged $11,000 a year, for a company with annual sales of $30–100 million. There was no evidence introduced to demonstrate that the corporation was harmed by the payments or that the funds were used for illegal bribes. A shareholder suit on these facts would probably not produce an adjudication of liability for breach of the duty of care. At best, such a case would be settled for a small fee paid to the plaintiff's attorney and the corporation's promise to follow better internal controls to ensure that such action did not recur. Nor do the *Siegel* defendants appear to have been prosecuted for violation of the disclosure requirements of the securities laws in the twenty-count indictment. Perhaps the prosecutor recognized that the sums in question were so trivial that their nondisclosure would not be material, and if that came out at trial, it could undermine the prosecution on other charges. The best explanation for such a bizarre use of prosecutorial resources is that the case was intended to pressure corporate defendants into implicating union officials for prosecution and not to vindicate shareholder rights.[71] In a strongly worded dissent, Judge Ralph Winter succinctly stated what was wrong with the prosecution and the court's affirmance of it: it created a "new crime—corporate improprieties—which entails neither fraud nor even a victim."[72]

A byproduct of criminalizing fiduciary duties is, then, the shifting of the regulation of the conduct of corporate officers and directors from state to national jurisidiction. When the Supreme

---

69. Coffee, "Does 'Unlawful' Mean 'Criminal'?" p. 202.

70. 717 F.2d 9 (2d Cir. 1983).

71. See Ralph K. Winter, "Paying Lawyers, Empowering Prosecutors, and Protecting Managers: Raising the Cost of Capital in America," *Duke Law Journal*, vol. 42 (1993), p. 945.

72. United States v. Siegel, 717 F.2d at 24 (Winter, J., dissenting).

Court attempted to stem the prosecutorial bootstrapping of the mail and wire fraud statutes in 1987 by requiring, in contrast to cases like *Siegel*, deprivation of property for action to constitute a scheme to defraud under the federal statutes in *McNally v. United States*,[73] Congress reversed it. It enacted a statutory definition, one year after *McNally*, that included defrauding "another of the intangible right to honest services," thereby reviving the standard that the Supreme Court had rejected and thus the likelihood of more prosecutions like *Siegel*.[74]

As Jack Coffee notes, a problem with this legal development is that Congress has overlaid a paradigm of criminal law on top of civil law without considering whether the civil law standard should be backed by the threat of criminal sanctions.[75] Coffee contends that

---

73. 483 U.S. 350 (1987).

74. 18 U.S.C. § 1346 (1988). The Supreme Court also quickly backtracked on its contraction of mail fraud statute jurisdiction in its holding that confidential business information could be intangible property in Carpenter v. United States, 484 U.S. 19 (1987). As Coffee explains, this decision undermined McNally, because prosecutors could simply relabel what was indictable as deprivation of an intangible right pre-McNally as deprivation of intangible property post-Carpenter. Coffee, "Does 'Unlawful' Mean 'Criminal'?" p. 205.

75. Coffee, "Does 'Unlawful' Mean 'Criminal'?" p. 206. There has also been a parallel trend criminalizing negligence in what Jack Coffee terms the technicalization of crime, in which administrative and statutory obligations, such as disclosure regulations under federal environmental and securities laws, are provided with both civil and criminal sanctions, including vicarious criminal liability for corporate officers. Thus, officers have been criminally indicted for failure to follow correct maintenance and safety procedures required by Federal Aviation Administration regulations, United States v. Eastern Air Lines (filed, E.D. N.Y. July 25, 1990); criminally prosecuted and convicted in what were traditionally considered civil violations in the securities law area, such as stock parking (a reporting and record-keeping violation for hiding the true ownership of shares), United States v. Mulheren, conviction reversed by the Second Circuit in 938 F.2d 364 (1991); and held vicariously criminally liable for having a responsible share in the furtherance of a transaction (rodent contamination in a warehouse in violation of the federal Food, Drug, and Cosmetic Act) even when they attempted to prevent the violation, United States v. Park, 421 U.S. 658 (1975). Coffee applies the same objections discussed in the text to these developments, for they involve actions that are neither intentional nor avoidable by careful conduct; for instance, as he puts it, workplace injuries and disposal of toxic wastes are inevitable outputs of legitimate professional

criminalization of such actions is undesirable because it diminishes the importance of blameworthiness as the foundation of our criminal law and lends itself to arbitrary and discriminatory treatment. But the key difficulty with the criminalization of fiduciary duties from the perspective of this monograph is that it nationalizes state corporate law. Such a development withdraws fiduciary duty law from the dynamic force of state competition. This is unfortunate, for the essence of good corporate law is adaptability to changing business conditions; there is no reason to suppose that federal prosecutors and courts respond to incentives as state courts and legislators do in this area. In fact, fiduciary duty law has changed significantly over time as business practices and governance arrangements have changed. By the 1960s, for instance, restrictions on self-dealing transactions had been loosened from the turn-of-the-century rule that contracts with interested directors were voidable at the instance of the corporation or shareholders, to their being valid unless found unfair by a court.[76] In the 1980s, directors' liability for damages for breach of the duty of care has been limited, eliminated, or made optional.[77]

An equally important destructive consequence of the criminalization of fiduciary duty law is the undermining of the efficacy of state competition by removing interpretive issues of fiduciary duty law from state control. Conduct that a state would not define as a breach of fiduciary duty can still subject a manager to liability in a bootstrapping criminal action under the federal mail and wire fraud statutes. This possibility, that state law does not determine managers' fiduciary obligations to shareholders, diminishes the value of a statutory domicile. Furthermore, as Judge Ralph Winter has observed, the expansion of criminal liability surely increases the cost of capital for firms, as investors are not the principal beneficiaries of the prosecutions, which may be brought to pressure corporate managers into

---

activities in modern industrial society. Coffee, "Does 'Unlawful' Mean 'Criminal'?" p. 219.

76. For a discussion of the evolution of the duty of loyalty (self-dealing restrictions), see Robert C. Clark, *Corporate Law* (Boston: Little, Brown & Co., 1986), pp. 160–71.

77. For a review of the recent changes in directors' and officers' liability and the duty of care, see Roberta Romano, "Corporate Governance in the Aftermath of the Insurance Crisis," p. 1155.

implicating third parties, such as union leaders, prominent investment bankers, and public officials, in criminal activity.[78] Federal criminalization of fiduciary conduct is therefore a disturbing development: its full effects will be understood only after we have more experience with the courts' reaction in this unfolding area.[79]

---

78. Winter, "Paying Lawyers, Empowering Prosecutors, and Protecting Managers."

79. Courts may interpret the new statutory definition of mail and wire fraud narrowly in corporate fiduciary cases. In the parallel development of the criminalization of regulatory violations, federal courts have sometimes thrown out the convictions.

117

6
Explaining American Exceptionalism

STATE COMPETITION FOR CORPORATE CHARTERS is unique to the United States. This chapter examines American exceptionalism in corporate law by contrasting the legal rules, institutions, and corporate ownership patterns of other federal systems, Canada and the European Community, that impede a state or nation-state's ability to exercise effective jurisdiction over firms, thereby preventing corporate charter competition. Although Canada has a federal system—firms can incorporate in one of ten provinces or under the Canada Business Corporations Act as a national corporation—an active market for corporate charters has not developed. Similarly, the Treaty of Rome envisions a federal system for the European Community, with its integrated economic market, but it has not fostered corporate charter competition among EC members, despite concerns by corporate law commentators that it would.

The chapter concludes by considering a theme in the popular press with implications for corporate law, the declining rate of growth of U.S. productivity relative to other nations. The best available evidence on productivity growth rates indicates that the concern is, in fact, misconceived. More important for the issues involved in this monograph, the relative decline in the growth rate of U.S. productivity over the past several decades cannot readily be ascribed to differences in corporate governance regimes.

Production of Corporate Law in Canada

There are two interesting studies of corporate charter competition in Canada, a pioneering study by Ronald Daniels and a careful critique of it by Jeffrey MacIntosh.[1] Daniels contends that enactment of the

---

1. Ronald J. Daniels, "Should Provinces Compete? The Case for a Competitive

118

Canada Business Corporations Act provoked a competitive reaction by provinces, creating uniform code provisions, similar to the situation in the United States.[2] MacIntosh disagrees, maintaining that the diffusion of the CBCA across the provinces is a function of the preferences of the administrators who initiate corporate law reform, rather than charter competition: administrators either strongly prefer uniform laws or develop a consensus view on what constitutes a good law.

Daniels develops his thesis by showing that the role of the Canadian national government in charter competition has been analogous to Delaware's: besides the rapid diffusion of CBCA reform provisions across the provinces, the predominant choice of reincorporating firms is national.[3] Many firms also initially incorporate under the CBCA, with the bulk coming from businesses located in one province, Quebec. Daniels suggests that this phenomenon is a function of special political concerns and incorporation fee structure. Changes in incorporation levels across the two regimes (Quebec and Canadian) are related to the growing political success of the separatist party in Quebec and to changes in franchise fees. Quebec's fees are calculated on a scale graduated according to a firm's capital, which imposes a higher charge than other provinces and the CBCA, which assess a small flat fee.[4] In 1985, national incorporation fees were increased from $200 to $500 (Canadian); thereafter national incorporations by Quebec firms slowed, and the total number of national

---

Corporate Law Market," *McGill Law Journal*, vol. 36 (1991), p. 130; Jeffrey MacIntosh, "The Role of Interjurisdictional Competition in Shaping Canadian Corporate Law: A Second Look," University of Toronto Law and Economics Working Paper 18 (Toronto, 1993).

2. Daniels, "Should Provinces Compete?" pp. 151–55. The national corporation statute was introduced in 1975. Daniels does not indicate the reason for this enactment (that is, whether firms or regulators were dissatisfied with provincial regimes). He does note that the national government sought provincial input into the drafting process but because the provinces were reluctant to participate, it acted unilaterally; ibid., p. 151 n. 49.

3. Ibid., pp. 152, 157, 165 n. 69. Moreover, like the development of Delaware's code, some of the Canadian government's reforms in the CBCA had previously been enacted by provinces; ibid., p. 154.

4. Ibid., pp. 167–69. Other provinces abandoned graduated fee systems by the beginning of the 1980s.

incorporations decreased. Presumably, by 1985, with the union still intact, the Quebec business community was less concerned over the separatist movement, so that price became the determinative factor in an incorporation decision. Recent events reviving the issue of separation (the rejection in 1992 of a proposed constitutional provision concerning Quebec's distinctive status) may induce a reversion to national incorporation.

Canada's 1985 fee increase, Daniels suggests, had a political source: Quebec politicians lobbied for a national fee increase to improve their market share of incorporations.[5] He does not, however, address why the national government acceded to such a request. If the national government was competing for corporate charters, then it is difficult to explain why it acquiesced to Quebec's lobbying for higher national incorporation fees. In fact, this datum seems to provide evidence that the national government was not seriously attempting to compete with the provinces, consistent with MacIntosh's view of Canadian corporate law reform, which treats the innovative features of the CBCA as either a random event or a function of bureaucratic preferences rather than a response to corporate demands.

Alternatively, the national government might have been competing for charters, but administrators thought that they offered a sufficiently superior product that firms would be willing to pay a premium for a national domicile, just as U.S. firms are willing to pay higher franchise fees for a Delaware address. Such an explanation—miscalculation of the price sensitivity of firms—is not compelling, however, because the government did not respond to the significant decline in incorporations after the rate change with a rate reduction to recoup its market position. Another explanation that partially reconciles Daniels's and MacIntosh's competing views of the Canadian charter market is that, whatever its motivation when it adopted the innovative CBCA, the national government simply decided to stop competing for charters when it decided to raise incorporation fees: presumably Quebec was willing to provide the national government with greater benefits than it received from charter revenues, such as support on policy issues unrelated to corporate law, in compensation for the franchise fee revision.

---

5. Ibid., pp. 168–69. None of the provinces raised their fees in response to the national fee increase.

Whether or not spurred by Quebec's lobbying, the national government's fee increase underscores the feebleness of a national government's incentive to compete for charters. A national government's ability to commit itself credibly to a responsive corporation code is limited, despite pioneering efforts at corporate law reform, because firms understand that such a government faces a minimal financial penalty from failure to continue to innovate. Franchise fee revenues are an insignificant percentage of a national government's budget.[6] Hence, such a government is far less motivated than a small state, such as Delaware, to be responsive to firms. The decrease in national incorporations after the fee increase is, then, not simply a function of the sensitivity of firms to charter prices. Rather, it is a function of price and an additional factor, the government's reputation for responsiveness. Action with an adverse effect on the government's reputation will reduce the number of new incorporations, as will an increase in price. In this scenario, firms perceived the national government's fee increase as an indication that it would also capitulate to provincial pressure concerning substantive code content. As a consequence, national incorporations declined as firms realized that it was too costly to run the risk of a national domicile.

To bolster this explanation for the decrease in national incorporations, it would be useful to know whether there were contemporaneously important national issues on which Quebec's support was key and which led to the increase in the national government's incorporation fee. Quebec's desire for separation may have been one such issue: if raising the CBCA incorporation fee disproportionately subsidized Quebec because it was the only province losing corporate revenues under the old rate structure, then the change could route

6. A crude estimate, providing an order of magnitude, can be extrapolated from Daniels's data on new incorporations under the CBCA and Canada's gross domestic product; ibid., pp. 158, 160 (tables 2 and 3). In 1988, the national government earned approximately $6 million in fees from new incorporations, compared to approximately $4 million in 1984; these amounts are less than 0.5 percent of Canada's gross domestic product. MacIntosh indicated that at the current fee level the national government obtains $6 million from franchise fees, an amount equal to 1/25,000 of the national budget; MacIntosh, "Role of Interjurisdictional Competition," p. 11. He further suggested that were the national government to recruit an incorporation business more actively, the additional revenues would still be insignificant, amounting to approximately 1/10,000 of the national budget.

additional national funds to Quebec and mollify separatist impulses. It certainly would be plausible for a national government to place priority on preserving the union over maintaining a reputation as a reliable sovereign for corporations, especially given the infinitesimal revenues that it obtained from corporate chartering.

Daniels concludes that state competition is far less effective in Canada than in the United States, and MacIntosh contends that it does not exist, because several factors important to Delaware's success are lacking, in particular the development of a comprehensive and specialized corporate law jurisprudence, as well as a significant dependence on franchise revenues. The best explanation for the more limited Canadian competition for charters, which both Daniels and MacIntosh emphasize, is that provinces do not control their corporation codes: authority is shared with independent provincial regulators and national judges. In particular, securities law administrators, whose jurisdiction is based on the residence of the investor rather than on the domicile of the issuing firm, are able to regulate corporate governance and thereby override provincial corporate law regimes.[7] The Ontario Securities Commission, for example, imposes fiduciary obligations on majority shareholders under its public interest powers.[8] Securities commissions also regulate shareholder communications, going-private transactions, attendance at shareholder meetings, and receipt of financial statements.[9] As long as a firm has a shareholder in Ontario (a probable event, as it is the most populous province), its corporate law can be dictated by the Ontario Securities Commission rather than the legislature or court of its province of incorporation. This authority has even been exercised over stock transactions involving solely non-Ontario investors.[10] In the United States, by contrast, the Supreme Court has refused to expand the reach of the national securities laws to include traditional fiduciary duties, and it has preserved the states' jurisdiction over corporate governance even in the one area of overlapping jurisdiction,

---

7. Daniels, "Should Provinces Compete?" pp. 182–84.

8. Ibid., p. 183 n. 119.

9. MacIntosh, "Role of Interjurisdictional Competition," p. 30.

10. Ronald J. Daniels and Jeffrey G. MacIntosh, "Toward a Distinctive Canadian Corporate Law Regime," *Osgoode Law Journal*, vol. 29 (1991), pp. 1, 37.

takeover regulation.[11] The Securities and Exchange Commission has also been prevented by the courts from forays into corporate governance.[12]

In addition, the Supreme Court of Canada reviews all provincial appellate courts.[13] This feature of jurisdictional spillover may be less important than the activities of securities law administrators, however, for Daniels states that in recent years the Supreme Court of Canada has reviewed few provincial decisions involving corporate or commercial matters.[14] Business appeals became discretionary in 1974, when the automatic appeal right for cases whose amount in controversy exceeded $10,000 was eliminated and the court's docket changed considerably, as constitutional cases increased throughout the 1980s with the adoption of the Canadian Charter of Rights and Freedoms.[15] Still, in the United States there is little if any basis for the U.S. Supreme Court to review a Delaware court's corporate law decision.

A further difference between the United States and Canada affecting corporate law jurisdiction is that all Canadian judges are federal appointees with life tenure. As MacIntosh notes, even a province that sought to create a special corporate law court along the lines of Delaware cannot do so as effectively as Delaware: the provincial judicial nominees must be appointed through a national process, which is not conditioned on the provincial government's approval.[16] In addition, life tenure diminishes the judge's incentive, provided by the need for reappointment, to be responsive to changing business conditions. Thus, the ability of Canadian provinces to deliver a predictable and stable corporation code like Delaware is

---

11. Santa Fe Industries v. Green, 430 U.S. 462 (1977); CTS Corp. v. Dynamics Corp. of America, 481 U.S. 69 (1987).

12. Business Roundtable v. SEC, 905 F.2d 406 (D.C. Cir. 1990) (striking down SEC regulation of shareholder voting).

13. Daniels, "Should Provinces Compete?" pp. 186–87.

14. Ibid., p. 187 n. 132 (from 1986 to 1989, only 14 of 304 cases heard by the Canadian Supreme Court could be classified as corporate or commercial).

15. Ibid., p. 187.

16. MacIntosh, "Role of Interjurisdictional Competition," p. 37.

attenuated further, because they do not exercise complete control over judicial appointments.

A province's control over what is ostensibly its substantive law and the judges who interpret that law is, then, highly circumscribed. This weakens the incentive to invest in assets that maintain a responsive corporate law regime because the value of such assets can be dramatically impaired by the actions of securities regulators in other provinces or by the Canadian judiciary.[17] The inability of provinces to commit credibly to a responsive corporate law regime, given overlapping jurisdiction, also renders firms less willing to invest in optimizing incorporation decisions, which has a feedback effect, further reducing provincial incentives to compete.

A second important distinguishing institutional feature, besides control of the code, contributes to the difference in competition for charters between the United States and Canada. Large Canadian corporations have greater concentration of stock ownership than their U.S. counterparts. Daniels and MacIntosh note that more than half the firms in the Toronto Stock Exchange 300 Composite Index are owned by a single shareholder with holdings exceeding 50 percent of the votes, whereas only 12 percent of the U.S. Fortune 500 firms are controlled by a 50 percent shareholder or shareholder group.[18] As ownership concentration increases, the choice of legal regime declines in importance: management with voting control does not need statutory discretion to operate a firm because it has the votes to change statutory default rules as it pleases. A firm with a concentrated ownership structure is therefore not likely to pay a premium

17. I have no explanation for why Canadians tolerate such interference in corporate governance by securities administrators; neither Daniels nor MacIntosh provides one. To the extent that provincial securities administrators cannot discriminate against foreign-incorporated firms, the overlapping jurisdiction problem may be mitigated if all provinces are interested in charter revenue maximization: top provincial authorities could rein in their securities administrators from rendering decisions that undercut the province's corporation laws, and other provinces' laws would, derivatively, be protected. Overlapping oversight still adds unnecessary friction to a competitive system, which may slow the introduction and diffusion of corporate law reforms, as one province's innovation may run into difficulty with administrators in another province that has yet to adopt the reform provision.

18. Ronald J. Daniels and Jeffrey G. MacIntosh, "Capital Markets and the Law: The Peculiar Case of Canada," *Canadian Investment Review*, vol. 3 (1990), pp. 77, 80–81.

willingly for a corporate law regime that is superior on several Delaware dimensions, such as organizational flexibility and managerial discretion.

Self-dealing issues are, however, more important from the public shareholders' perspective when ownership is concentrated than when it is diffuse. If insiders need outside equity capital, they then have an incentive—a lower cost of capital—to incorporate in a province whose regime best protects minority interests against self-dealing. But this involves a far more limited area of corporation laws on which provinces could compete in comparison with U.S. law, and thus even vigorous Canadian charter competition would be more circumscribed than that of the United States.

Jurisdictions such as Canadian provinces that are populated by firms with concentrated stock ownership, then, have less to gain from corporate charter competition than those whose firms are more widely held, such as U.S. states. Hence, any economic return from provincial competition for chartering would be far lower than the return in the United States. Causality, however, could run in the opposite direction: in the absence of vigorous competition for corporate charters, equity investments of public firms could become more concentrated, as investors compensate for less responsive legal regimes with more immediate monitoring of management. We do not have data to test the direction of causality in the relation between corporate ownership and charter competition, and I am uncertain whether an adequate test could be constructed.

Differentiation of which shareholder issues matter when ownership composition varies is borne out in a comparison of the two countries' shareholder litigation rules. Shareholder litigation is more easily undertaken in the United States than Canada. Canada follows the British cost rule, in which a losing party pays the other's costs (costs follow the event), although the losing plaintiff-shareholder in a derivative suit can petition the court for indemnification from the corporation.[19] Furthermore, contingent fees are not as prevalent in Canada; they are not permitted in Ontario, require local bar society

---

19. See Frank H. Buckley and Mark Q. Connelly, *Corporations: Principles and Policies*, 2d ed. (Toronto: Emond Montgomery, 1988), p. 615; Jeffrey G. MacIntosh, "The Oppression Remedy: Personal or Derivative?" *Canadian Bar Review*, vol. 70 (1991), pp. 29, 56.

approval in other provinces, and are legislatively capped, typically at 25 percent.[20] In addition, class action rules, following British procedure, are more restrictive than in the United States.[21] The Canadian cost and class action rules severely restrict the incentive for a shareholder to bring a lawsuit against management, an incentive that is weak to begin with, because litigation costs typically exceed the plaintiff's pro rata benefit. The U.S. solution to the collective action problem of shareholder litigation is to create an incentive for attorneys, who are paid on a contingent fee basis, to bring shareholder suits by offering the prospect of recovery of a substantial legal fee from the defendant corporation.[22] The Canadian rules eliminate the U.S. solution.

Why don't Canadian provinces seek to compete in the dimension of lawsuit accessibility, as U.S. states do? One explanation is that greater concentration of ownership affects litigation patterns and reduces the need for more accommodating access rules. In particular, controlling shareholders have superior incentives to monitor managers for breach of the duty of care[23] compared with dispersed shareholders

---

20. I would like to thank Jeffrey MacIntosh for explaining to me how contingency fees are used in Canada.

21. Unlike U.S. class actions, the British rules require that an amount in liquidated damages be specified and that class members have identical claims. These requirements discourage suits. Consequently, most shareholder suits that are not brought under the derivative statutes are individual (personal) actions. There is, however, proposed legislation in Ontario to change class action rules; Quebec has, in fact, departed from the British practice. The greater difficulty in pursuing a class action may not be as consequential as it appears. Canadian securities administrators have much greater discretion than the SEC in affecting firms' governance, so shareholder claims that in the United States are pursued as class actions may be undertaken, at the government's expense, by securities regulators in Canada. I would like to thank Jeffrey MacIntosh for explaining these differences to me.

22. See John C. Coffee, "The Unfaithful Champion: The Plaintiff as Monitor in Shareholder Litigation," *Law and Contemporary Problems*, vol. 48 (1985), p. 5. As Coffee and others have detailed, there are serious problems with such an incentive scheme, including conflict of interest between shareholders and attorney and the possibility of frivolous litigation.

23. See Romano, "The Shareholder Suit," pp. 81–82 (U.S. firms with lower management stock ownership sued more frequently for breach of duty of care, whereas those with high management stock ownership more frequently sued for breach of duty of loyalty).

with small holdings, and their managers rarely engage in unilateral action to thwart a takeover because firms with controlling owners are not subject to hostile bids. Two common categories of U.S. shareholder suits are therefore of little concern to the vast majority of Canadian firms.[24] This reduces the need for increased access to the courts.

A less efficiency-centered explanation of Canadian shareholder litigation rules is that controlling shareholders and their counsel have exerted influence on Canadian corporation codes to obtain laws that make shareholder litigation difficult in order to enrich themselves at the minority's expense. This, however, is not a persuasive explanation because, in contrast to U.S. corporation codes, Canadian codes have statutory oppression remedies, which entail simplified filing procedures compared with derivative and individual (personal) shareholder actions in the United States. These provisions are aimed at providing relief against corporate action detrimental to the minority.[25] Moreover, if provinces are not competing for charters in the first place, this would also answer the question why they do not compete on the dimension of lawsuit accessibility, without need of recourse to a controlling shareholder–political conspiracy explanation.

The Canadian experience is not clearly analogous to the close corporation context in the United States, where charter competition is arguably anemic; Canadian firms differ significantly from U.S. close corporations. In contrast to close corporations, Canadian corporations with concentrated ownership are publicly traded, and thus stock market signals are available to price the legal regime for the minority shareholders. In addition, Canadian firms with controlling owners are typically much larger than U.S. close corporations. They are consequently more likely to engage in repetitive transactions for which the product of charter competition—standard form contracts—is of value.

There is, however, a simpler answer to the claim that there is little competition for corporate charters in Canada compared with the United States than the story developed thus far. Such an explanation

---

24. Ibid., p. 60.

25. For a discussion of the oppression remedy, and the extent to which courts have interpreted it to cover derivative claims, see MacIntosh, "The Oppression Remedy." MacIntosh is skeptical of the efficacy of the remedy.

involves numbers: there are far fewer provinces than states, and industrial organization theorists conventionally link competition to market structure (that is, number of producers as well as barriers to entry).[26] Although there are five times as many states as provinces, the credible commitment explanation of Delaware's success, built on transaction-specific assets that create a reputation for responsiveness, suggests that competition is viable only for a subset of states, those small enough for franchise revenues to make a budgetary difference. Accordingly, it is questionable whether the smaller number of provinces accounts for the absence of vigorous competition, as opposed to the barrier created by overlapping jurisdictional authority and the more limited demands placed on corporation codes because of the concentration of equity ownership of publicly traded Canadian firms.

Production of Corporate Law
in the European Community

The EC federal system provides an important comparison with the U.S. and Canadian regimes. The Treaty of Rome established as a goal a common European economic market.[27] Coordination of economic policies was essential to achieve this goal, but a strong central government was eschewed. The treaty established instead the aim of harmonizing corporate laws across the EC.[28]

Although EC economic integration aims have been analogized to the commerce among U.S. states in an American common market,[29]

---

26. The earliest work along these lines is associated with Joe Bain. See Jean Tirole, *The Theory of Industrial Organization* (Cambridge: MIT Press, 1988), p. 1.

27. This goal has since been reformulated to achieve an even broader economic and political union among a larger group of European nations than the original signatories.

28. Treaty of Rome, March 25, 1957, Rome, 298 U.N.T.S. 11, art. 54 3(g). Harmonization is achieved by means of directives, which are issued by the institutions of the EC (Commission and Council of Ministers) and are addressed to, and binding on, the member states, although each nation is free to choose, through its own implementing legislation, how to achieve the directive's required results. Slaughter and May, "The European Community," in *European Corporate Finance Law* (London: Euromoney Publications, 1990), pp. 9, 10.

29. See Edmund Kitch, "Regulation and the American Common Market," in A. D. Tarlock, ed., *Regulation, Federalism, and Interstate Commerce* (Cambridge, Mass.:

the U.S. approach to corporate law has not been emulated. To the contrary, European commentators frequently justify corporate law harmonization as a mechanism for ensuring that a European Delaware will not emerge.[30] These commentators either concur in Cary's characterization of Delaware as a pariah state or recognize that some European nations pursue, through their corporation codes, objectives other than shareholder wealth maximization and that such policies can be sustained only if there is no charter competition.

Most European nations take what is referred to as an enterprise approach to the corporation, which requires the representation of employees as well as shareholders in corporate decision making. The German code, for instance, establishes a system of two-tiered corporate boards, termed codetermination, in which workers are represented on the firm's supervisory board, which appoints the managing board handling day-to-day operations; other nations, such as the Netherlands, mandate different forms of worker participation including rights to receive information, to nominate board members, and to be consulted on important decisions.[31] As the interests of employees

Oelgeschlager, Gunn and Hain, 1981), p. 9; Richard M. Buxbaum and Klaus J. Hopt, *Legal Harmonization and the Business Enterprise* (Berlin: de Gruyter, 1988), p. 7; Eric Stein, *Harmonization of European Company Laws* (Indianapolis: Bobbs-Merrill, 1971), p. 59.

30. See, for example, Christian Timmermans, "Methods and Tools for Integration," in R. Buxbaum, G. Hertig, A. Hirsch, and K. Hopt, eds., *European Business Law: Legal and Economic Analysis on Integration and Harmonization* (Berlin: de Gruyter, 1991), pp. 129, 132–33; Johan de Bruycker, "EC Company Law—The European Company v. The European Economic Interest Grouping and the Harmonization of the National Company Laws," *Georgia Journal of International and Comparative Law*, vol. 21 (1991), pp. 191, 193; K. Van Hulle, "The Harmonisation of Company Law in the European Community," in *Harmonization of Company and Securities Laws: The European and American Approach* (Tilburg: Tilburg University Press, 1989), p. 10; David Charny, "Competition among Jurisdictions in Formulating Corporate Law Rules: An American Perspective on the 'Race to the Bottom' in the European Communities," *Harvard International Law Journal*, vol. 32 (1991), p. 423. For consistency, I continue to use the term "corporate law" although the conventional terminology is "company law," following U.K. usage.

31. See Clark D. Stith, "Note, Federalism and Company Law: A 'Race to the Bottom' in the European Community," *Georgetown Law Journal*, vol. 79 (1991), pp. 1581, 1588–89 n. 25; Buxbaum and Hopt, *Legal Harmonization*, p. 180. Worker participation entered into European corporation codes in the mid-1970s. Buxbaum and Hopt, *Legal Harmonization*, pp. 260–61. Its German roots are, however, far

and shareholders differ—workers' claims are fixed, while shareholders are the residual claimants on a firm's cash flow, who are paid after all fixed claims are met—maximization of share value is unlikely to be the objective of corporations operating under enterprise-oriented legal regimes. Some commentators, for example, attribute Volkswagen's financial difficulties to labor's alliance on the supervisory board with the largest shareholder, the state government, which fostered a "politics of jobs" that prevented the firm from cutting costs compared with its international rivals.[32]

It is questionable whether such worker representation provisions enhance shareholder value. If they did, one would expect U.S. states and firms to opt for such arrangements: the powerful dynamic of state competition ensures that provisions perceived to increase share value are enacted over time. Interestingly enough, although the German model of a two-tiered board is available to French firms, almost none have adopted it.[33] Some U.S. states and firms have adopted other-constituency statutes and charter provisions, takeover provisions that

---

more ancient. Because worker participation is not a feature of U.K. corporate law, the fifth directive on corporate governance (comprising minimum standards on corporate board composition and employee participation) has produced the greatest controversy in the harmonization of corporation laws; it was first drafted twenty years earlier and is not likely to be adopted in the near future; Frank Wooldridge, *Company Law in the United Kingdom and the European Community* (London: Athlone Press, 1991), p. 80. Indeed, the latest draft seems to give up on attaining a consensus and permits member states to choose from various models of governance to retain their diverse solutions; Buxbaum and Hopt, *Legal Harmonization*, p. 203. Buxbaum suggests that the difference in corporation law objectives is related to the difference in choice of law rule: the common law or Anglo-American tradition that narrowly defines corporate internal affairs as relations between managers and shareholders "leads more readily than does the broader [European] enterprise law concept to the use of the contractually fixable state of incorporation, rather than to the more objectively set siège social as the reference point for a corporate conflicts of laws rule"; Richard Buxbaum, "The Origins of the American 'Internal Affairs' Rule in the Corporate Conflict of Laws," in J. Musielak and K. Schurig, eds., *Festschrift für Gerhard Kegel zum 75. Geburtstag 26 Juni 1987* (Stuttgart: W. Kohlhammer, 1987), pp. 75–76.

32. See Ferdinand Protzman, "Volkswagen Sees Need for Shake-up," *New York Times*, March 15, 1993, pp. D1, D8.

33. Klaus J. Hopt, "Directors' Duties to Shareholders, Employees and Other Creditors: A View from the Continent," in E. McKendrick, ed., *Commercial Aspects of Trusts and Fiduciary Obligations* (Oxford: Clarendon Press, 1992), pp. 115, 116.

have a surface resemblance to the European rules, but are distinctive in practice. As noted, these U.S. provisions permit directors to consider employee interests in decisions regarding control changes but do not require such consideration, and employees have no right to enforce a provision, let alone any specific representation or participation rights. [34]

A further institutional difference complicates the analysis of the objectives of German firms. German corporations do not independently fund their pension commitments through investments in securities, as U.S. firms do. Rather, they accumulate balance sheet reserves, retaining earnings and investing internally. Some scholars view this practice as justification for codetermination: workers have a long-term claim on the firm, their pensions, which warrants representation on the board. [35] Such pensions are still fixed claims, however, and not residual claims analogous to an equity interest in the firm. Not only must pension commitments be insured under German law, but shareholders, not workers, bear the risk of poor management because pensions are debts that must be paid whether or not internal reserves are adequate. Other commentators suggest a different connection between codetermination and German pension practice. In their view, the unfunded pension arrangement is necessary to safeguard the balance in board membership created by codetermination: if German pension funds were invested in stock, then the supervisory board's balance would be tilted even more toward labor than at present because employees could appoint directors beyond their statutory allotment as a group, through the votes of their pension fund shares. [36] Recalibration of statutory requirements of codetermination boards on implementation of a pension policy funded similarly to U.S. firms through stock investments is not perceived by these commentators to be a viable political option. These competing

---

34. See Hansen, "Other Constituency Statutes"; Romano, "Corporate Governance," pp. 1164–65.

35. See Friedrich Kubler, "Institutional Investors and Corporate Governance; A German Perspective" (paper presented at the University of Osnabrück conference on institutional investors and corporate governance, July 1992).

36. See Michael Hauck, "The Equity Market in Germany and Its Dependency on the System of Old Age Provisions" (paper presented at the University of Osnabrück conference on institutional investors and corporate governance, July 1992), p. 11.

explanations of the relation between pension fund investments and codetermination indicate that the objective of German corporations is difficult to characterize and may well not be maximization of equity share prices.

Nations pursuing mixed objectives in corporation codes cannot compete effectively for corporate charters (at least not in a race to the top) against states whose codes focus on shareholders: stock values of firms incorporated in the former nations will be lower than those in the latter, where firms will prefer to locate. Financial capital is far more mobile than labor, and the higher capital costs of a nonshare value-maximizing regime will therefore not be sufficiently offset by lower labor costs in a firm's decision calculus. To preserve multiple objective codes, nations will therefore seek to prevent the emergence of an active charter competition: the absence of competition ensures the viability of their corporation laws. The EC's harmonization process achieves such a goal. Harmonization need not eliminate competition entirely,[37] but, by mandating a floor, it severely reduces the returns from innovation and, correspondingly, from competition.

Quite apart from normative concerns over state competition and the harmonization effort, there are a number of legal and institutional barriers to an active European market for corporate charters. The most important barrier is the prevailing choice-of-law rule: except for the United Kingdom and the Netherlands, European nations follow the law of a company's real or effective seat (*siège réel*) rather than of statutory domicile (registered office).[38] Reincorporation is far more, if not prohibitively, expensive under a real seat rule than under a statutory domicile rule, because physical assets (a firm's headquarters) must be relocated to change legal regimes. The greatest expense of such a move is probably not the cost of new facilities but rather that of relocation of human capital. Despite the goals of integration, cultural differences across EC member states are still pronounced,

---

37. See Stith, "Note, Federalism and Company Law"; Timmermans, "Methods and Tools for Integration," p. 140 (the Netherlands "legislator has sometimes refused to go further than the minimum level required by company law directives arguing that otherwise Dutch business would be disadvantaged in its competition with companies from other Member States").

38. Timmermans, "Methods and Tools for Integration," p. 133.

and it is consequently problematic whether top management would be willing to move or commute to another country.[39]

Moreover, under both the real seat rule and the British statutory domicile rule, reincorporation is far more expensive than in the United States because a transfer of the registered office is treated as a liquidation and the firm is taxed on hidden reserves (that is, asset appreciation).[40] Reincorporations are not taxable events under U.S. tax laws.

Changing legal regime is therefore quite difficult, if not prohibitive, for European firms. The incentives to be responsive to innovations in corporate law in order to increase the number of domestic incorporations are, correspondingly, weak, if not nil. In fact, Richard Buxbaum suggests that the real seat rule originated in efforts to prevent competition: in the nineteenth century, when the United Kingdom became what he terms a European Delaware, French corporations were prevented from taking advantage of the U.K. law by changes in doctrine regarding corporate seat.[41]

There are several additional roadblocks to competition for corporate charters, but, in contrast to the real seat rule, these can be more easily overcome by a nation that desires to improve its charter business, whether or not other nations choose to compete. First, European nations do not impose annual franchise taxes.[42] Virtually all European countries, however, tax stock transactions and the issuance of shares and impose filing fees on initial incorporations.[43]

---

39. Europeans are generally less mobile than U.S. citizens. See "U.S. Regions Offer Lessons for the EC," *Wall Street Journal*, August 3, 1992, p. 1.

40. Wooldridge, *Company Law*, p. 8. The tax can be avoided if the government approves the transfer of the company's headquarters. Andreas Reindl, "Companies in the European Community: Are the Conflict-of-Law Rules Ready for 1992?" *Michigan Journal of International Law*, vol. 11 (1990), pp. 1270, 1278. Such transactions are also taxed in real seat regimes.

41. Buxbaum, "Origins of the American 'Internal Affairs' Rule," pp. 85–86.

42. See CCH, *Doing Business in Europe* (Chicago: CCH, 1993); Walter H. Diamond and Dorothy B. Diamond, *Capital Formation and Investment Incentives around the World* (New York: Matthew Bender, 1991).

43. See CCH, *Doing Business in Europe*; Diamond and Diamond, *Capital Formation*. Since 1990, three European countries, Germany, the Netherlands, and the United Kingdom, have abolished stock transfer taxes. Colin Jamieson, "Stamp Duties in the European Community: Harmonization by Abolition?" *British Tax*

If incorporations do not generate an annual source of revenue, then there is little incentive for a nation to compete to obtain such business. In contrast to the real seat rule, this is not a true barrier to charter competition. The real seat rule's obstacle to competition cannot be eliminated by one nation adopting a statutory domicile rule because it requires mutual recognition across nations to be effective. One nation could, however, offer a superior code in exchange for payment of an annual incorporation fee and, like Delaware, attract firms by offering a superior product that reduces the cost of doing business, making payment of an annual fee worthwhile, even if other nations do not impose such fees. Moreover, because all nations impose initial incorporation fees, there is a source of revenue that will increase on offering a responsive code, even without adopting an annual charge.

Second, it is far more difficult for shareholders to sue directors and officers in Europe than in the United States or Canada. Representative actions, derivative or class, are not generally permitted under European corporate laws, and contingent fees are prohibited in most European countries.[44] Institutions essential to shareholder litigation in the United States are therefore missing from the European legal landscape. In addition, fiduciary doctrines are not as well developed in Europe as in the United States. Continental legal systems, for example, do not appear to have the concept of the trust on which such duties rely: France, for instance, does not have a corporate opportunity doctrine, which prevents managers from taking, for personal profit, business opportunities that are offered to the corporation, and the duty of loyalty is generally less well-developed in France and Germany than in the United States.[45] Given such circum-

---

Review, vol. 9 (1991), p. 318. Although a directive eliminating this tax was proposed in 1976 and revived in 1987, there was no concern when these nations acted that the EC would adopt the directive; rather, the source of the reform was competition for stock exchange business; ibid.

44. Buxbaum and Hopt, *Legal Harmonization*, pp. 215–17. Buxbaum and Hopt indicate that the EC Commission has proposed articles, in the draft fifth directive, that would require member nations to permit shareholder derivative suits.

45. André Tunc, "Corporate Law," in R. Buxbaum, G. Hertig, A. Hirsch, and K. Hopt, eds. *European Business Law: Legal and Economic Analysis on Integration and Harmonization* (Berlin: de Gruyter, 1991), pp. 199, 211–12; Buxbaum and Hopt, *Legal Harmonization*, p. 184; Hopt, "Directors' Duties to Shareholders," p. 127.

stances, shareholder litigation is an event of extremely low probability, and differences in legal regimes will correspondingly be less important to both managers and investors.[46] Accordingly, nations' incentives to compete for incorporations on many crucial corporate law dimensions are attenuated. This phenomenon does not explain why one nation does not enact rules more accommodating to shareholder litigation, as current EC harmonization efforts do not appear to block such a strategy, although the conflicts of law and tax burden discussed earlier severely curtail a nation's ability to capture, and profit from, a substantial market share of EC incorporations.

Shareholders without a lawsuit option for disciplining management will demand other mechanisms to protect their interests or else will pay less for their investment. European nations could presumably compete on such alternative dimensions. Compared with U.S. corporation codes, however, shareholders' rights are more attenuated in other dimensions as well. Rights of inspection of company books and records are not universal.[47] In addition, shareholder voting rights are more frequently restricted in Europe than in the United States.[48] A common strategy employed by German corporations, for instance, is to limit the number of shares that a shareholder can vote.[49] Absence of competition in these other governance dimensions, however, may be related to the dearth of litigation. Delaware's success is due not simply to a superior corporation code but also to the development of a rich body of case law that assists firms' corporate planning. Without a steady stream of lawsuits creating precedents to interpret code provisions, the attractiveness of a jurisdiction as a corporate domicile is diminished. This problem would be compounded by a jurisdiction's concomitant lack of judicial expertise, as the dearth of cases would not make it worthwhile for judges to become knowledgeable in

---

46. See Romano, "Law as a Product," for a discussion of the importance of litigation in state competition.

47. See Stephen M. Davis, *Shareholder Rights Abroad: A Handbook for the Global Investor* (Washington, D.C.: Investor Responsibility Research Center, 1989); Stith, "Note, Federalism and Company Law," pp. 1587–88 n. 24, 1593–94.

48. Ibid.

49. See "In Defense of Voting Restrictions," *Financial Times*, June 12, 1992; Theodor Baums, "Banks and Corporate Control," University of Osnabrück Working Paper 91–1 (Osnabrück, 1991).

corporate law. It may therefore not be worthwhile to engage in a vigorous corporate charter competition when shareholder litigation is not a viable option. A nation could expend effort at improving its code but still not attract a substantial number of incorporations: a poorly developed case law, without any prospect for improvement, would make corporate planning difficult, as the boundaries of permissible action are unknown.

Differences regarding shareholder rights aid in explaining why there is no European competition for corporate charters, but such an explanation begs the question of why this is the situation. Why don't European nations adopt U.S. litigation, shareholder rights, and other governance procedures and thereby profitably compete for incorporations? To repeat a tired refrain, difficulties of attracting businesses because of the real seat rule is surely part of the answer. But another institutional factor helps to explain the absence of competition, involving a feature that also distinguishes Canada from the United States, differences in corporate ownership patterns. A striking characteristic of European capital markets is their undercapitalization when compared with U.S. markets: market capitalizations are a far smaller percentage of European nations' economies.[50] U.S. stock market capitalization is approximately 50 percent of gross national product, whereas the corresponding European figures are far lower:[51] it is approximately 20 percent for Germany and 24 percent for France. (Table 6–1 provides comparative market data.)

In many European nations, such as Germany and France, corporate capital is raised privately through banks and not in the capital market,[52] a process that helps to explain the thinness of their equity markets. Whether control is held by families or banks, stock ownership of European corporations is more concentrated than that of U.S. or U.K. firms.[53] Ninety percent of European takeovers,

---

50. Solnik, *International Investments*, pp. 99–101, 120; Gabriel Hawawini, *European Equity Markets: Price Behavior and Efficiency*, Monograph 1984–4 (New York: Solomon Brothers Center, New York University, 1984), pp. 21–24.

51. Solnik, *International Investments*, p. 99.

52. Ibid., p. 101.

53. See, for example, Mike Wright, Ken Robbie, and Steve Thompson, "Corporate Restructuring, Buy-outs, and Managerial Equity: The European Dimension," *Jour-*

TABLE 6–1
COMPARATIVE DATA FOR CAPITAL MARKETS, SELECTED COUNTRIES,
1988

Country	Value[a]	Volume[b]	Concentration[c]	GDP[d]
United States	2,481	1,356[e]	.14	4,840.2
United Kingdom	718	166	.22	845.5
West Germany	241	174	.42	1,176.7
France	224	69	.25	939.5
Canada	221	68	.24	505.9
Switzerland	148	n.a[f]	.49	178.5
Italy	135	31	.45	836.1
Spain	87	28	.47	354.0
Netherlands	86	30	.72	224.8
Belgium	58	11	.53	152.2

a. Market capitalization value in billions of U.S. dollars.
b. Total value of share turnover in billions of U.S. dollars on major exchanges.
c. Concentration (percent of market capitalization) of ten largest firms.
d. Gross domestic product in billions of U.S. dollars.
e. New York Stock Exchange volume only.
f. Data not available.
SOURCES: Bruno Solnik, *International Investments*, 2d ed. (New York: Addison-Wesley, 1991); International Monetary Fund, *International Financial Statistics (Yearbook)* (Washington, D.C.: IMF, 1991).

contested or otherwise, occur in the United Kingdom, for example, because of differences in capital markets: other European capital markets are less developed, require less corporate disclosure, and are dominated by banks and insurance companies as shareholders.[54]

As noted in the Canadian context, it is difficult to test empirically whether charter competition has contributed to the great depth

---

nal of Applied Corporate Finance, vol. 3 (Winter 1991), p. 46. The difference is evident in the absence of an active market for corporate control in Europe compared with the United States and United Kingdom; Wright, Robbie, and Thompson, "Corporate Restructuring"; Marlene Givant Star, "LBOs Take Global Tilt," *Pensions and Investment Age*, August 7, 1989, pp. 37, 38.

54. Comment of Geoffrey Fitchew, in R. Buxbaum, G. Hertig, A. Hirsch, and K. Hopt, eds., *European Business Law: Legal and Economic Analysis on Integration and Harmonization* (Berlin: de Gruyter, 1991), p. 375.

of U.S. capital markets compared with European nations or whether the depth of the capital market fosters charter competition.[55] The interrelation is important because governance needs differ across firms with concentrated or diffuse equity ownership. Competition for charters is less important for privately held than public corporations, because differences in corporate law regimes are not as significant to such firms: owners are few in number and have voting control and hence can run a firm without serious constraint. Agency problems between managers and shareholders are therefore less likely in such firms than in publicly traded companies with diffuse stock ownership. More important, in contrast to the Canadian setting where most large corporations have concentrated equity ownership, there is no comparable market discipline for many European firms, because they are not publicly traded. Hence, a key feedback mechanism that provides information to investors and drives state competition—share prices— is missing in the European context.

The relatively small number of publicly traded European corporations, compared with the United States and Canada, is balanced by a substantial number of large privately held firms. This distinctive pattern in choice of business form is a function of the search for more flexible organizational forms by European firms that appears to be analogous to the search for more advantageous corporation codes by U.S. corporations. That is, there appears to be a European genus of state competition, which involves choice of business form rather than choice of incorporation state. The number of limited liability or private companies in Germany and Belgium, for instance, has grown much more rapidly in recent years than publicly traded corporations.[56] Limited liability companies are corporations that cannot

---

55. The distinctive practice concerning German pensions noted earlier may also affect the liquidity of German capital markets: pension funds, which are the largest players in many other nations' equity markets, have no demand for German equity; Hauck, "Equity Market in Germany." If pension assets are used for internal projects because capital markets are less developed, then charter competition might lead to a redirection of pension assets outside the firm. It is, however, probable that many German managers would continue to engage in internal project financing through pension assets to avoid the discipline imposed by external capital markets.

56. Buxbaum and Hopt, *Legal Harmonization*, pp. 171–73 (Germany); Eddy Wymeersch, "Groups of Companies," in R. Buxbaum, G. Hertig, A. Hirsch, and K. Hopt, eds., *European Business Law: Legal and Economic Analysis on Integration*

issue stock that is publicly traded; they are distinct legal entities subject to different and less restrictive codes than public corporations. Competition over choice of business form is more limited in scope than American-style charter competition, for the choice of form entails forgoing access to capital markets. But this may not be too costly a trade-off for European firms, given the thinness of European capital markets.

Commentators contend that businesses choose the limited liability corporation to avoid the more onerous regulation imposed on public corporations, such as higher taxes, more extensive worker participation regimes, and more rigid legal requirements.[57] The most important regulatory restraint for comparative purposes is the rigidity of corporate law rules for public corporations. The bulk of worker participation rules typically cannot be avoided by choice of business form: they apply to all enterprises with a specified number of employees.[58] Some of Germany's largest corporations are, in fact, limited liability companies. In contrast, in the United States privately held corporations that choose to obtain different default rules by

---

and Harmonization (Berlin: de Gruyter, 1991), pp. 227–28 (Belgium). Although the significance of an increasing use of the private corporation form by European firms can be overstated—new incorporations of closely held corporations also outpace that of public corporations in the United States, because most new businesses are small-scale enterprises—it is an important phenomenon because, as discussed in the text, most such U.S. firms do not opt into the special close corporation statutes and instead choose the same corporate law regime as public firms.

57. Buxbaum and Hopt, *Legal Harmonization*, p. 171; Wymeersch, "Groups of Companies," p. 228; Angel Rojo, "The Typology of Companies," in R. Drury and P. Xuereb, eds., *European Company Laws* (Aldershot, Eng.: Dartmouth Publishing Company, 1991), pp. 41, 44–45 (German public companies diminishing in numbers because of tax law and rigidity in legal form, which, unlike private company rules, cannot be tailored to firm needs).

58. This is not true in all cases. To attract the business of international holding companies, the Netherlands exempts such corporations from its worker participation regime. The exemption is not inconsistent with domestic labor's being the principal influence on the regime: holding companies and small-scale businesses have few production employees, and, hence, as their internal organization is not of concern to labor unions, their exemption from the regulatory regime is acceptable to the unions. This suggests that the transposition of charter competition over choice of domicile into competition over choice of corporate form may be caused by the mixed objectives of European corporation codes (that is, they do not take maximization of share value as the goal of the firm).

opting into a state's close corporation statute must meet statutory limits on the number of shareholders and are therefore small businesses. No large U.S. firms are incorporated under a close corporation statute, and only a few are privately held. The best explanation for this difference, again, is the powerful motivation of participants in business to select the wealth-maximizing legal regime from among the menu of alternatives, however sparse the menu.

Is There a Relation between Productivity and Corporate Governance?

The legal and institutional differences across the United States, Canada, and Europe make it difficult to ascertain whether one approach to corporate law is superior to another. But a repeated theme of commentators is that European, as well as Japanese, corporate governance arrangements with more concentrated stock ownership, particularly by financial institutions, compared with U.S. firms are superior because in certain sectors those nations' firms have been more successful competitors than their U.S. counterparts. Some commentators locate the failure not in the federal system of state competition but rather in national legislation restricting the stock ownership of financial institutions.[59] The implication, regardless of the statutory source of concern, is that the predominant corporate governance arrangements of foreign firms are preferable to those of U.S. firms and that the United States ought to adjust its corporation laws and other laws shaping corporate governance such as the Glass-Steagall Act, which prohibits stock ownership by banks, to match those of other nations. Because there are no comparative empirical studies showing that corporate governance arrangements affect productivity, the position hinges on the significance attributed to other nations surpassing the United States on a variety of productivity growth measures in recent years. For instance, growth in productivity measured by GDP per capita from 1870 to 1979 was 691 percent for the United States but 1,396 percent for Germany, and 1,653 percent for Japan; as measured by the growth rate in GDP per work-hour from

---

59. For example, Mark J. Roe, "A Political Theory of American Corporate Finance," *Columbia Law Review*, vol. 91 (1991), p. 10; Michael E. Porter, *The Competitive Advantage of Nations* (New York: Free Press, 1990).

1970 to 1979, it was 1.92 for the United States, 4.5 for Germany, and 5.03 for Japan.[60] The debate focuses on relative growth rates because in absolute productivity the United States has retained its lead.

The most comprehensive study of productivity to date, by William Baumol, Sue Anne Batey Blackman, and Edward Wolff, shows that the significance of differences in short-term productivity growth rates has been vastly overblown.[61] They make several important points about productivity measures that are critical to understanding their significance. First, productivity growth rates are extremely volatile in the short run and hence are best estimated over long periods. Second, the lag in the rate of U.S. productivity growth compared with other nations is a long-standing phenomenon, going back a century, and is not of recent vintage, as critics suggest. Third, the decline in U.S. productivity in recent years is only a comparative decline: it is a decrease compared with the phenomenal spurt in U.S. productivity following World War II. The current growth rate is, in fact, similar to the historic U.S. normal growth rate. The extraordinary increase in postwar U.S. productivity growth equals (and thus can be seen to compensate for) the steep decrease in productivity growth during the Great Depression. When a growth trendline is computed, U.S. productivity has remained constant from 1880 through 1980. Moreover, *all* industrial nations have experienced the same temporal pattern of productivity growth rates, an unusual postwar increase and a slowdown during the 1970s. Fourth, and most important, short-run productivity differences are not indicia of economic decline because of the phenomenon of international convergence. When one nation's productivity is superior to that of many other economies, those nations that are not too far behind can

---

60. William J. Baumol, Sue Anne Batey Blackman, and Edward N. Wolff, *Productivity and American Leadership: The Long View* (Cambridge: MIT Press, 1989), pp. 13, 88.

61. The data and analysis in the following paragraphs are taken entirely from the Baumol, Blackman, and Wolff study, *Productivity and American Leadership*, especially from pp. 14, 65, 68–71, 89–90, 258–60. This study is particularly interesting because it is a reversal of the authors' earlier critical assessment of U.S. productivity performance in William Baumol and Kenneth McLennan, eds., *Productivity Growth and U.S. Competitiveness* (New York: Oxford University Press, 1985).

catch up, as they learn from the leader through technology transfer. Performance levels thus converge. The laggard countries have more to learn from the leader than the leader from them, and consequently "those who were initially behind *must* advance more rapidly than those who were ahead. Otherwise the distance between them could not possibly narrow."[62] Baumol, Blackman, and Wolff exhaustively detail the evidence supporting the international convergence thesis.

More recent work, including a productivity measure update through 1990 by Baumol and Wolff and a study of service sector productivity by McKinsey and Company, reinforces the Baumol, Blackman, and Wolff study's assessment of the significance of productivity growth rates and indicates that absolute U.S. productivity has continued to exceed that of Europe and Japan.[63] Baumol and Wolff's latest data on manufacturing performance, for example, indicate that the rate of productivity growth in Germany has, in fact, been slower than that of the United States for more than a decade (a decline predating economic difficulties brought on by reunification) and that Japan's productivity growth rate has slowed down considerably and is now not much greater than that of the United States, while the Japanese level of productivity is still far lower than the U.S. level.

After reviewing findings of other studies of superior U.S. productivity in the manufacturing sector, the McKinsey study provides five case studies in the service sector (airlines, retail banking, restaurants, general merchandise retailing, and telecommunications). Because it is difficult to measure the performance of a service industry (the value of output is not always quantifiable), the study examines a variety of labor productivity measures. It finds that, in each sector, labor productivity is higher in the United States than in Europe or Japan. The superior performance of U.S. firms is attributed to the greater domestic competition these firms face.

The lower productivity growth rate of the United States compared

---

62. Baumol, Blackman, and Wolff, *Productivity and American Leadership*, p. 90 (italics in original).

63. William J. Baumol and Edward N. Wolff, "Comparative U.S. Productivity Performance and the State of Manufacturing: The Latest Data," in *CVStarr Newsletter* of New York University Center for Applied Economics, vol. 10 (1992), p. 1; McKinsey Global Institute, *Service Sector Productivity* (Washington, D.C.: McKinsey & Co., October, 1992). The McKinsey study received assistance from several distinguished economists: Martin Baily, Francis Bator, and Robert Solow.

with that of Europe and Japan in the postwar period is therefore best understood as a manifestation of the inevitable catch-up entailed by international convergence. We do not have to introduce differences in corporate governance regimes to explain differences in performance. This explanation of changing relative rates of productivity growth does not imply that low relative productivity growth is not a public policy concern. The hard question for public policy is whether another nation will eventually surpass the United States because the long-term historic U.S. growth rate is not sufficient to retain world economic leadership. While we have no way of predicting whether the United States will be surpassed as the economic leader, the answer will not be found in mimicking other nation's corporate governance arrangements. The key factors that economists believe affect absolute productivity performance are the national savings rate (investment), the education of the labor force, and the magnitude of efforts devoted to basic and applied research:[64] there is no evidence of a relation between any of these three factors and corporate governance rules. Commentators concerned about the effect of corporate governance on comparative economic performance do not emphasize and sometimes do not even mention these key factors. The omission is probably not as odd as it appears: there is no theory or evidence relating these fundamental factors to corporate governance patterns.

Moreover, the disparate corporate governance systems that commentators treat as significantly related to performance—U.S. firms have dispersed stock ownership; European firms have concentrated ownership and, in Germany, heavy bank involvement; and Japanese firms have extensive corporate cross-holdings of equity, forming corporate groups[65]—were all in place before World War II, well before the postwar years in which the steep relative decline in U.S. productivity has been identified.[66] In conjunction with the Baumol,

---

64. Baumol, Blackman, and Wolff, *Productivity and American Leadership*, pp. 258–60.

65. There are two types of Japanese corporate groups, financial keiretsu, which consist of groups of firms linked by relationships to a main bank, and enterprise keiretsu, which consist of firms centered on a particular enterprise, like Toyota. The firms in the groups have strong product-market links in addition to cross-equity holdings.

66. In the prewar years from 1870 to 1929, there is no discernible pattern between

Blackman, and Wolff data, this institutional detail indicates that changes in the rate of growth in productivity cannot be directly attributed to differences in corporate governance structure.

The point of this review of the comparative productivity literature is not to endorse existing U.S. restrictions on active equity investment by financial institutions. Indeed, such regulation ought to be repealed to permit greater experimentation with corporate governance and ownership structures; repeal is the policy most consistent with the enabling structure of competitive state corporation codes, which enhances firm value, as this monograph has emphasized. The point is rather that the desirability of such reform does not, and should not, stem from preoccupation with U.S. competitiveness, and that the common belief of the comparative failure of U.S. business is a canard. If improved relative performance is the goal, it is inappropriate to try to force U.S. corporations to adopt the internal organization of other nations' firms. U.S. firms are, in fact, more productive than their competitors in nearly all sectors, and we ought to approach any reform efforts with that central fact as the point of reference.

A variety of anecdotes from U.S. history and other nations is relevant to a reconsideration of U.S. rules restricting corporate ownership by financial institutions, although this evidence does not make the effect on corporate governance of such ownership reform easy to predict. A fascinating study by J. Bradford De Long indicates that, at the turn of the century, adding a Morgan banker to a corporate board increased stock value by 30 percent.[67] De Long finds no evidence that public investors were exploited by Morgan: companies with a Morgan director sold at higher multiples of book value than other companies, and stock offering prices and subsequent rates of return were comparable to non-Morgan companies.[68] Although Morgan was engaged in both commercial and investment banking at the

corporate governance form and productivity growth rate. The U.S. rate surpassed that of Japan in all years but 1890–1900 and 1913–1929 and that of Germany in all years but 1880–1900; Baumol, Blackman, and Wolff, *Productivity and American Leadership*, p. 88. Stockholdings had already become diffuse compared with German and Japanese firms in this period.

67. J. Bradford De Long, "Did J. P. Morgan's Men Add Value? An Economist's Perspective on Financial Capitalism," in P. Temin, ed., *Inside the Business Enterprise* (Chicago: University of Chicago Press, 1991), p. 205.

68. Ibid., pp. 223–24.

time, De Long's data do not indicate what positions, if any, as owner or creditor Morgan had in the companies on whose boards its partners served. In addition, De Long cannot determine whether the source of the value added by a Morgan banker is that of effective corporate governance (that is, that the market viewed a Morgan appointment as a screen for corporate quality, as an active monitor who would protect firm value) or of monopoly rents (that the market perceived the appointment as an indicium that the firm would be able to create a monopoly through business interconnections that now would be established with other Morgan firms). Thus, De Long's data are suggestive, rather than conclusive, that repeal of the Glass-Steagall Act would improve corporate governance and thereby enhance share value.

Alfred Chandler's recent comprehensive study of the modern industrial corporation provides a contrary example concerning the impact of financial institutions' involvement in corporate governance. Chandler chronicles the development of the largest industrial corporations across the most dynamic industries in the United States, Germany, and Great Britain: the corporations that invested in production, distribution, and management capabilities established first-mover advantages that led to their domestic as well as international dominance in industry share.[69] As Chandler notes, one of the initially successful firms in its industry, United States Steel, is "one of the very few examples of banker control in American industry."[70] Yet, unlike the other first movers in his study, U.S. Steel lost its early leading position because of poor management. As one reviewer states, "Chandler leaves little doubt that he believes that the financiers and lawyers running U.S. Steel made serious mistakes."[71]

One would be hard pressed to make predictions from these two contradictory anecdotes concerning the effect of repealing the Glass-Steagall Act on share value. Another interesting study of early American banking by Naomi Lamoreaux further muddies the water.

---

69. Alfred D. Chandler, Jr., *Scale and Scope: The Dynamics of Industrial Capitalism* (Cambridge: Belknap Press, 1990).

70. Ibid., p. 139.

71. David J. Teece, "The Dynamics of Industrial Capitalism: Perspectives on Alfred Chandler's Scale and Scope," *Journal of Economic Literature*, vol. 31 (1993), pp. 199, 205 n. 12.

Lamoreaux's research suggests that U.S. banks might not adopt the active investor role of German and Japanese banks even if the option were made available. Nineteenth-century New England banks voluntarily exited from arrangements similar to those of German and Japanese bankers—ones in which banks lend to insiders with interlocking bank and corporate managerial positions and actively monitor and influence borrowers' behavior—and instead engaged in financial intermediation; the new arrangements were undertaken for efficient risk-reduction reasons.[72] Thus, at least in one region of the United States, the divorce of private bankers and industrialists began long before it was required by federal statute.

This pattern of banks not exercising control over industrial corporations is reinforced by contemporary comparisons abroad. As Jack Coffee has noted, U.K. firms are not subject to U.S.-type ownership restrictions, yet they have dispersed stock ownership rather than a bank-dominated governance structure.[73] This difference may be a historical accident, that is, it may be due to disparate industrial development in England and Germany in the late eighteenth and early nineteenth centuries that led to the establishment of different financial institutions.[74] But whatever the reason for the difference, it makes plain that regulatory barriers are not a sufficient explanation for U.S. governance structures. Indeed, in contrast to the American legal regime, Japanese regulation prohibited the development of capital markets, forcing corporations to rely on bank financing. When the restrictions were loosened in the 1980s, there was a dramatic shift away from bank debt to public debt.[75]

---

72. Naomi Lamoreaux, "Information Problems and Banks' Specialization in Short-Term Commercial Lending: New England in the Nineteenth Century," in P. Temin, ed., *Inside the Business Enterprise*, p. 161.

73. John C. Coffee, "Liquidity versus Control: The Institutional Investor as Corporate Monitor," *Columbia Law Review*, vol. 91 (1991), p. 1277.

74. See Richard Tilly, *Financial Institutions and Industrialization in the Rhineland, 1815–1870* (Madison: University of Wisconsin Press, 1966), pp. 134–35; Alexander Gerschenkron, *Economic Backwardness in Historical Perspective: A Book of Essays* (Cambridge: Belknap Press, 1962).

75. Bank debt of public corporations declined from 90 percent in 1975 to less than 50 percent in 1992. Takeo Hoshi, Anil Koshyap, and David Scharfstein, "The Choice between Public and Private Debt: An Analysis of Post Deregulation Corporate Financing in Japan" (unpublished manuscript, University of Chicago and MIT, 1993).

These examples suggest that it would be a mistake to maintain that U.S. corporate governance institutions are best understood as political and not economic (that is, efficient). A more useful way to characterize the connection between politics and economic organizational form, particularly in the contractual context of business organization, is to recognize that private parties are persistent in devising institutions that circumvent or minimize the effect of political constraints on economic development.[76] The genius of American corporate law in this regard is that the dynamics of state competition reduces the number of extraneous regulations that must be bypassed.

---

76. See, for example, Tilly, *Financial Institutions and Industrialization in the Rhineland* (detailing how Rhenish bankers and entrepreneurs created financial mechanisms that circumvented the Prussian government's restrictions on their economic development).

7

Conclusion

THE MAKING OF AMERICAN CORPORATE LAW is unique among federal political systems: state competition has produced innovative corporation codes that quickly respond to changing market conditions and firm demands. Corporate law commentators have long debated whether this responsiveness is for the better. The best available evidence indicates that, for the most part, the race is for the top and not the bottom in the production of corporation laws. But the direction of corporate law reform is not linear. The adoption of state takeover statutes, which have adverse effects on shareholder wealth, demonstrates that state competition is far from perfect; so may rules facilitating shareholder litigation. Perfection, however, is not the proper yardstick for measuring the legislative output of state competition: the time frame of analysis is more important. In the short run, there will inevitably be deviations from the optimum in a federal system. But in the longer run, competitive pressures are exerted when states make mistakes, as in the example of the vast majority of firms exiting from much of Pennsylvania's takeover regime. Such self-correcting pressure is absent in a centralized national system. There is no reason to believe that where state laws are inadequate, a national corporation law would be better, and there is, indeed, some reason to believe that it would be worse.

The answer to the question of the efficacy of state competition is therefore between the polar positions of Winter and Cary, albeit far closer to the Winter (that is pro–state competition) than to the Cary (that is, pro–federal regulation) end of the continuum, given the numerous event studies surveyed throughout this monograph. One implication of the analysis is that investors and public policy are best served by detailed examination of the effects of specific statutes on shareholder welfare rather than rhetorical debate over the appropriate sovereign for corporations, for there is no reason to support federal regulation. Another implication is that the default regime for coverage by new code provisions for which there is a discernible conflict of interest between managers and shareholders, such as takeover statutes, should be an opt-in one. That would ensure that coverage would be decided by those who bear the cost of a value-decreasing charter provision, while at least partially neutralizing management's advantage over challengers in the proxy process by requiring management, and not shareholders, to commence the amendment process. A final implication concerns the mandatory federal laws that regulate securities transactions, at best with inconclusive efficacy; we should open these laws to experimentation by making them optional at the shareholders' choice. Such a policy is consistent with the wealth-increasing, enabling approach of state corporation codes. Finally, the trend to federal criminalization of fiduciary duties should be stopped; apart from the general policy question concerning the appropriateness of criminal sanctions for torts, particularly questionable violations, it undermines the essence of state competition, autonomy of the incorporation state over manager-shareholder relations.

Competition for incorporation revenues makes U.S. states sensitive to investor concerns: such competition is the genius of American corporate law. Lacking complete control over their corporation laws, Canadian provinces apparently have not engaged in charter competition. With no similar financial incentives and legal barriers to reincorporation, European nations have maintained corporation codes that promote mixed objectives. The EC's harmonization process further sustains the adoption of these codes. This is exemplified by the persistent effort in the EC's harmonization effort to require employee participation in corporate governance (the proposed fifth directive), an effort to mandate provisions that do not emerge in a competitive corporate law regime, for neither U.S. states nor firms have opted for such governance structures. Concerns over the emergence of a European Delaware are, from the shareholders' perspective, profoundly misplaced, since state competition for charters in the United States has, on balance, benefited shareholders, while harmonization may have a deleterious effect on their interests. One possible consequence, or possible cause, of the lack of charter competition in Canada and Europe is the more concentrated stock ownership of their large corporations compared with U.S. firms. A

149

legal regime may be of less significance to a controlling shareholder, compared with dispersed owners, for the former can implement policies (he has the votes) and will not need legal mechanisms to aid in monitoring firm performance (he runs the firm and can oust poorly performing managers).

There is no evidence that charter competition has hurt the comparative economic performance of U.S. firms. Productivity is higher in the United States than in Europe or Japan. In addition, differences in relative productivity growth are, in all likelihood, a function of international convergence, the process by which techno- logical innovation diffuses across nations, from leader to followers. U.S. firms' comparative economic performance has sometimes been raised as an issue to question both state corporation codes and U.S. federal laws that impose restrictions on corporate equity ownership of financial institutions, which differ from European and Japanese legal regimes.

While the comparative productivity data do not support repeal of the federal statutes in question, let alone a change in state codes, the data on the market for corporate charters, which is the focus of this monograph, do go to the issue: the benefits from experimentation in the choice of institutional form, afforded by state competition, suggest that similar benefits would result from experimentation in corporate governance arrangements by repealing ownership restric- tions. Given the experience in the United Kingdom and in the banking industry in nineteenth-century New England, however, as well as recent trends in Japanese corporate finance, repeal will not necessarily make U.S. corporations look more like those in Europe and Japan, where banks have considerably more influence in corpo- rate governance.

Despite national differences in corporate governance, there is little to support the contention that U.S. institutions are simply a response to political rather than economic forces, and the corollary that as organizational forms they are inferior to other nations' insti- tutions. The effect of politics on business organization is far more subtle. The most accurate characterization of their interrelation is that of a constrained optimization problem, in which private parties design institutions that circumvent political constraints on economic activity. Although corporate managers may lobby for laws ensuring a quiet life and succeed in some instances, U.S. capital markets are remarkably resilient in devising ways to discipline them, such as the leveraged acquisitions of the 1980s. More important, the genius of American corporate law—the dynamics of state competition—limits the number of wealth-decreasing regulations that need to be finessed, thereby reducing the cost of doing business.

Board of Trustees

Paul F. Oreffice, *Chairman*
Former Chairman
Dow Chemical Co.

Edwin L. Artzt
Chairman and CEO
The Procter & Gamble
  Company

Winton M. Blount, *Treasurer*
Chairman
Blount, Inc.

Vaughn D. Bryson
President and CEO
Eli Lilly and Company

Joseph A. Cannon
Chairman and CEO
Geneva Steel Company

Raymond E. Cartledge
Chairman and CEO
Union Camp Corporation

Edwin L. Cox
Chairman
Cox Oil & Gas, Inc.

Christopher C. DeMuth
President
American Enterprise Institute

Malcolm S. Forbes, Jr.
President and CEO
Forbes Inc.

Tully M. Friedman
Hellman & Friedman

Christopher B. Galvin
Senior Executive Vice President
  and Assistant Chief Operating
  Officer
Motorola, Inc.

Robert F. Greenhill
Chairman and CEO
Smith Barney Shearson

Douglas Ivester
President
North American Business Sector
  Coca-Cola USA

James W. Kinnear
Former President and CEO
Texaco Incorporated

The American Enterprise Institute for Public Policy Research

Founded in 1943, AEI is a nonpartisan, nonprofit, research and educational organization based in Washington, D.C. The Institute sponsors research, conducts seminars and conferences, and publishes books and periodicals.

AEI's research is carried out under three major programs: Economic Policy Studies; Foreign Policy and Defense Studies; and Social and Political Studies. The resident scholars and fellows listed in these pages are part of a network that also includes ninety adjunct scholars at leading universities throughout the United States and in several foreign countries.

The views expressed in AEI publications are those of the authors and do not necessarily reflect the views of the staff, advisory panels, officers, or trustees.

Robert H. Malott
Chairman of the Executive Committee
FMC Corp.

George R. Roberts
Kohlberg Kravis Roberts & Co.

Edward B. Rust, Jr.
Chairman, President, and CEO
State Farm Mutual Automobile
  Insurance Company

Paul G. Stern

Wilson H. Taylor
Chairman and CEO
CIGNA Corporation

Henry Wendt
Chairman
SmithKline Beecham

James Q. Wilson
James A. Collins Professor
  of Management
University of California
  at Los Angeles

Charles Wohlstetter
Vice Chairman
GTE Corporation

Officers

Christopher C. DeMuth
President

David B. Gerson
Executive Vice President

Council of Academic Advisers

James Q. Wilson, *Chairman*
James A. Collins Professor
  of Management
University of California
  at Los Angeles

Donald C. Hellmann
Professor of Political Science and
  International Studies
University of Washington

Gertrude Himmelfarb
Distinguished Professor of History
  Emeritus
City University of New York

Samuel P. Huntington
Eaton Professor of the
  Science of Government
Harvard University

D. Gale Johnson
Eliakim Hastings Moore
  Distinguished Service Professor
  of Economics Emeritus
University of Chicago

William M. Landes
Clifton R. Musser Professor of
  Economics
University of Chicago Law School

Glenn C. Loury
Department of Economics
Boston University

Sam Peltzman
Sears Roebuck Professor of Economics
  and Financial Services
University of Chicago
  Graduate School of Business

Nelson W. Polsby
Professor of Political Science
University of California at Berkeley

Murray L. Weidenbaum
Mallinckrodt Distinguished
  University Professor
Washington University

Research Staff

Leon Aron
Resident Scholar

Claude E. Barfield
Resident Scholar; Director, Science
  and Technology Policy Studies

Walter Berns
Adjunct Scholar

Douglas J. Besharov
Resident Scholar

Jagdish Bhagwati
Visiting Scholar

Robert H. Bork
John M. Olin Scholar in Legal Studies

Michael Boskin
Visiting Scholar

Karlyn Bowman
Resident Fellow; Editor,
  The American Enterprise

David Bradford
Visiting Scholar

Dick B. Cheney
Senior Fellow

Lynne V. Cheney
W.H. Brady, Jr., Distinguished Fellow

Dinesh D'Souza
John M. Olin Research Fellow

Nicholas N. Eberstadt
Visiting Scholar

Mark Falcoff
Resident Scholar

Gerald R. Ford
Distinguished Fellow

Murray F. Foss
Visiting Scholar

Suzanne Garment
Resident Scholar

Patrick Glynn
Resident Scholar

Robert A. Goldwin
Resident Scholar

Gottfried Haberler
Resident Scholar

Robert W. Hahn
Resident Scholar

Robert B. Helms
Resident Scholar

Jeane J. Kirkpatrick
Senior Fellow; Director, Foreign and
  Defense Policy Studies

Marvin H. Kosters
Resident Scholar; Director,
  Economic Policy Studies

Irving Kristol
John M. Olin Distinguished Fellow

Michael A. Ledeen
Resident Scholar

Susan Lee
DeWitt Wallace–Reader's Digest
  Fellow in Communications
  in a Free Society

James Lilley
Resident Fellow; Director, Asian
  Studies Program

Chong-Pin Lin
Resident Scholar; Associate Director,
  Asian Studies Program

John H. Makin
Resident Scholar; Director, Fiscal
  Policy Studies

Allan H. Meltzer
Visiting Scholar

Joshua Muravchik
Resident Scholar

Charles Murray
Bradley Fellow

Michael Novak
George F. Jewett Scholar in Religion,
  Philosophy, and Public Policy;
  Director, Social and
  Political Studies

Norman J. Ornstein
Resident Scholar

Richard N. Perle
Resident Fellow

William Schneider
Resident Fellow

Bill Shew
Visiting Scholar

J. Gregory Sidak
Resident Scholar

Herbert Stein
Senior Fellow

Irwin M. Stelzer
Resident Scholar; Director, Regulatory
  Policy Studies

Edward Styles
Director of Publications

W. Allen Wallis
Resident Scholar

Ben J. Wattenberg
Senior Fellow

Carolyn L. Weaver
Resident Scholar; Director, Social
  Security and Pension Studies

*This book was edited by Ann Petty of the
publications staff of the American Enterprise Institute.
The text was set in Bodoni Book.
Coghill Composition Company of Richmond, Virginia,
set the type, and Edwards Brothers Incorporated,
of Ann Arbor, Michigan, printed and bound the book,
using permanent acid-free paper.*

The AEI Press is the publisher for the American Enterprise Institute for Public Policy Research, 1150 17th Street, N.W., Washington, D.C. 20036; *Christopher C. DeMuth,* publisher; *Edward Styles,* director; *Dana Lane,* assistant director; *Ann Petty,* editor; *Cheryl Weissman,* editor; *Mary Cristina Delaney,* editorial assistant (rights and permissions).

www.ingramcontent.com/pod-product-compliance
Lightning Source LLC
Jackson TN
JSHW011938131224
75386JS00041B/1433